# PRAISE FOR

M000198842

"In this charming, warm-hearted, often very funny book, Katie Burke takes us into the minds of children—a place we should all spend more time! Not only a wonderfully insightful kid's eye guide to San Francisco, *Urban Playground* is also an interactive manual for getting into the minds of your own—and your friends'—children. Reading its sweet—and sometimes quirky—interviews, is to see San Francisco with the freshest eyes possible."

**—JANIS COOKE NEWMAN**, author of *A Master Plan for Rescue*

"If you're seeking the honest truth from kids, you will find few better resources than *Urban Playground*, by San Francisco writer Katie Burke. Burke's StoryCorps-like interviews, quoting kids on everything from pupusas to Pride Week, reveal that the Bay Area remains a fertile ground for smart, confident, and fun-loving kids. Says a seven-year-old girl who's on the road to becoming an archaeologist, 'It usually takes about maybe a month or a year to dig up one dinosaur.' After reading this book, I wouldn't be surprised if she or another San Francisco kid figured out how to dig one up sooner!."

**—SALLY SMITH**, Editor and Co-Publisher, *The Noe Valley Voice*

"Children make the best tour guides. In Katie Burke's lively *Urban Playground* series, young city-dwellers share how they experience all aspects of city life, from restaurants, holidays, people, and parks to pets, schools, sports, shops, and activities. Their observations are moving and thought-provoking, and reveal what makes a city interesting and unique. This book will appeal to adults and kids who wish to see (and re-see) San Francisco."

**—CHRISTINA CLANCY**, author of *The Second Home*

"A fascinating peek into the minds of San Francisco's children. They are more insightful, creative and weird—in the best of ways!—than I'd ever imagined."

**—JULIA SCHEERES**, author of *A Thousand Lives*

"This delightful book of interviews of important San Franciscans—grade-school kids—works on so many levels. The wisdom of these children reveals what a great place San Francisco is to grow up in. As Willa notes, 'If it was medieval times, and San Francisco was a city with walls, we could still survive because we have everything we need.'"

—JOANNA BIGGAR, author of *Melanie's Song*

"San Francisco as seen through the eyes of its youngest denizens. More than just an insider's guide to places parents should take their kids in the city, Katie Burke's stories are a revelation about the lives, imaginations, and dreams of our future generation. Kids really do say the darndest things."

—SCOTT JAMES, journalist and author of
*San Francisco Chronicle* bestsellers *SoMa* and *The Sower*

"*Urban Playground* invites a multi-generational exchange on the joys and hardships of living in one of America's greatest cities. What makes this an important work is its honest recording of children's voices, their fears and dreams. It is a poignant reminder that family is defined in many ways."

—JOHNNIE BERNHARD, author of *A Good Girl*,
*How We Came to Be*, and *Sisters of the Undertow*

"With so much to see and do, it's easy for anyone to fall in love with San Francisco. Katie Burke's new book beautifully captures the wonder of this great city through the lens of San Francisco's most inquisitive residents—our children."

—RAFAEL MANDELMAN, San Francisco Supervisor, District 8

"Burke's writing captures the unique voice of each child she interviews, truly bringing to life the diversity of the city and giving the reader tons of ideas for things to do. Even if a trip to San Francisco isn't in the future, this book is still a fantastic resource for parents due to the discussion questions. I've used a couple of them with my own kids, and it's been eye-opening to hear their answers to questions I would have never thought to ask. Every city needs a book like this one, which allows reader of all ages to experience it through the eyes of a child."

—MEGAN HOLT, Ph.D., Executive Director of
One Book One New Orleans

# URBAN PLAYGROUND

# URBAN

*What Kids Say About*

# PLAYGROUND

*Living in San Francisco*

## KATIE BURKE

Published by SparkPress, a BookSparks imprint,
A division of SparkPoint Studio, LLC
Phoenix, Arizona, USA, 85007
www.gosparkpress.com

Published 2020
Printed in the United States of America
ISBN: 978-1-68463-016-5 (pbk)
ISBN: 978-1-68463-017-2 (e-bk)
Library of Congress Control Number: 2019919244

Interior design by Tabitha Lahr
Interior illustration page xii © Shutterstock
Map of San Francisco page x © iStockphoto
All other interior illustrations by Tim McGrath

To the children of San Francisco

# Contents

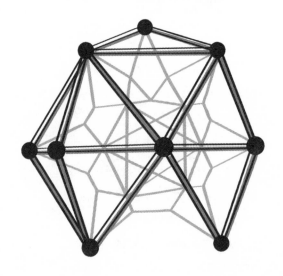

# San Francisco

PRESIDIO

SEA CLIFF

LAKE STREET

LINCOLN PARK

PRESIDIO HEIGHTS

JORDAN PARK / LAUREL HEIGHTS

LOW

PA

ANZA VIS

NORTH PANHAN

CENTRAL RICHMOND

INNER RICHMOND

LONE MOUNTAIN

OUTER RICHMOND

GOLDEN GATE PARK

HAIGHT ASHBU

BUEN

ASHBURY

COLE VALLEY / PARNASSUS HEIGHTS

INNER SUNSET

CLARENDON HEIGHTS

OUTER SUNSET

CENTRAL SUNSET

FOREST KNOLLS

MIDTOWN TERRACE

TWIN PEAKS

GOLDEN GATE HEIGHTS

FOREST HILL

INNER PARKSIDE

OUTER PARKSIDE

PARKSIDE

FOREST HILLS EXTENSION

DIAM HEIGH

WEST PORTAL

MIRALOMA PARK

SHERWOOD FOREST

PINE LAKE PARK

SAINTS FRANCIS WOOD

MERCED MANOR

MONTEREY HEIGHTS

WESTWOOD HIGHLANDS

SUNNYSIDE

BALBOA TERRACE

MOUNT DAVIDSON MANOR

WESTWOOD PARK

LAKESIDE

STONESTOWN

LAKE SHORE

INGLESIDE TERRACE

INGLESIDE

MISS

MERCED HEIGHTS

INGLESIDE HEIGHTS

OCEANVIEW

OUTER MISSION

CROC

# Author's Note

I interviewed the children featured in this book between July of 2018 and August of 2019. Each child's age listed in this book is as of the date of that child's interview, not as of the book release or any other date.

The profiles in this book contain quotes from my interviewees. Each quote is in the child's own words, except as occasionally edited for clarity. An "Insights from the Urban Playground" section in my voice follows each profile, to comment on certain aspects of city living from an adult perspective.

Following the "Insights" are five questions related to the child's profile, for children and their significant adults to discuss while reading the profiles together.

# Preface

In February 2017, my mom asked whether I wanted a Story-Worth subscription for my birthday, coming up in a week. Through StoryWorth, she explained, families wrote weekly stories to each other for a year, in response to questions from each other. Since I am both a writer and a person in love with my six nieces and two nephews, Mom reasoned, the kids should ask the questions, and I alone should answer them.

I accepted the mission, and over the course of the next year wrote fifty-three stories to Brennan, Maggie, Kenzie, Patrick, Elizabeth, Willie, Molly, and Abbey, then ages two to thirteen. I answered their questions, ranging from then-four-year-old Molly's "How do you like broccoli?" to this from Brennan, then thirteen: "What does Martin Luther King's legacy mean to you?"

The families received the stories online each week, and at the end, those comprised a three-volume set of hardcover books I entitled *Ask Aunt Katie*.

By the time I started this family project, I had been a writer for thirteen years. The sentence should read: Most of my recent writing had featured San Francisco, the city where

I have lived since 1999. *Ask Aunt Katie* was a love letter to the children in my life, just as San Francisco had captured my heart and pen in the writing that had come before.

After my StoryWorth year, I pursued another opportunity to publish writing for kids. I approached Sally Smith, one of the two founding and current editors of *The Noe Valley Voice*, a San Francisco neighborhood newspaper born in 1977, when I was three years old. Commonly called "Stroller Valley," Noe is a neighborhood full of kids that sits adjacent to my own neighborhood, Liberty Hill.

I said I'd love to write a monthly column for *The Noe Valley Voice*, and thus my career writing for and to kids in San Francisco began. In May 2017, we published the first installment of Kids Ask Katie, my monthly column, in which Noe Valley kids asked me questions about the neighborhood and I took them on field trips related to their question, then interviewed people who could help me answer it.

In one column, for example, ten-year-old Jasper Machule, who had recently moved to Noe Valley from the Mission neighborhood, asked me why Noe had fewer "abandoned people living on the streets" than the Mission did. He and I served breakfast to homeless people in the Mission, and homeless advocate Jennifer Friedenbach and Jeff Sheehy, who was then Supervisor of the district that includes Noe Valley, answered Jasper's question from their respective areas of expertise.

In 2018, I hired SparkPress Publisher Brooke Warner as my writing coach. After reading some of my stories about San Francisco and my letters to the children in my family and those of Noe Valley, Brooke helped me conceive this project—a book kids could read with their significant adults and learn about growing up in a city, whether they were themselves living in an urban center or had no idea what that would be like.

I instantly said yes to this project, which would bring together my love of kids and San Francisco. When I told my *Noe Valley Voice* editor, Sally, about this book project, she liked it so much that she suggested we change Kids Ask Katie to Noe Kids, a column in which I would ask Noe Valley kids about their lives. This time, it was my turn to ask the questions. In December 2018, Noe Kids made its debut with my profile of then-eleven-year-old Noe resident Ryker Fionn Rush.

In *Urban Playground: What Kids Say About Living in San Francisco*, fifty San Francisco kids, ages five to nine at the time of their interviews, tell readers about their lives in San Francisco through the lens of ten themes: family, food, heroes, holidays, pets, school, sports, talents, vacations, and work.

In these pages, San Francisco kids reveal everything from who lives at home with them to their career aspirations. They also share what thrills them about living in the city and what they think the bummers are.

I hope reading about these fifty characters is as much fun for you as talking with them was for me. May their words spark the curiosity of the children who read this book, connect its adult readers to their own childhoods, and reveal to all its readers what makes San Francisco such a special place to live.

# WHO IS IN
# YOUR FAMILY?

# Max, eight years old

Max, an eight-year-old boy in San Francisco, says his older sister is the funniest person in his family. He says, "She said this joke: 'How much dollars does it cost for a pirate to get his ears pierced?' And the answer was: 'A buccaneer.'"

Max has jokes too. For example: "How do you stop an astronaut's baby from crying?" he asked. "You rocket." Between his sister's jokes and his own, Max says he has many more jokes to tell.

Max says he has lots of chores. "At my mom's house, I have to take out the trash. In the morning, I have to get dressed, eat breakfast, brush my teeth, use mouthwash, floss, get ready to go to school, then go to school. At my dad's, I have to take the compost out and feed my dog," he says, referring to his chihuahua/mini-pinscher mix named Princess.

His favorite thing to do with his family is to play soccer. When at his mom's house, he plays at a nearby park that he calls "Library Park." When at his dad's, he plays at Alamo Square.

Max's least favorite rule at home is his 8:00 p.m. bedtime. "But I went to bed at 8:30 once," he says. "Mom doesn't know about that." He used the extra half hour to play with his toys.

Asked where he wants to live when he grows up, Max says, "I think I might want to buy a house in the Inner Richmond"—the neighborhood where he lives now—"because I want to live near my parents and visit them a lot."

ce⤳

Max will have pets when he is an adult. "I'm gonna buy this kind of frog, it's called a redwood frog, or a wood frog. I want to take it to Lake Tahoe because whenever it gets frozen, it has this chemical on its skin that defrosts it." Max will name his wood frog Duke.

Max will also have an iguana named Patrick, a parrot named Gobble, a puppy named Fred, and a kitten he will probably name Sophia. He will have a doggy door, an iguana door, and a "froggy door." Gobble can fly out the window to go outside, and the cat will use an indoor litter box.

Max will have two kids, Kevin and Emma. Emma will have lots of energy and be excited for everything, and she'll be good at math, soccer, and tennis. Max will teach Emma math when she's in kindergarten. Kevin will always be happy, and he'll be good at basketball, soccer, and baseball.

## Insights from the Urban Playground

San Francisco is a great place to learn jokes; there are people everywhere to tell you a funny one about buccaneers or why the chicken crossed the road. And there are lots of bookstores where families can buy joke books.

Your family can also find books about rare pets, like wood frogs, and learn how different animals handle cold climates. Maybe you could pick up a book of pet names!

San Francisco has many parks where kids can go looking for unusual animals and families can play soccer. There is usually good weather, making the city fun for energetic kids.

---

**DiSCUSSiON QUESTiONS**

1. Does anyone in your family tell funny jokes?
2. When you grow up, do you want to live near the family you're in now?
3. Would you want a wood frog for a pet?
4. Would you ever name an iguana Patrick?
5. Is anyone in your family good at both math and sports?

# Larkin, six years old

Larkin, a six-year-old girl, lives in Ashbury Heights with her mom, dad, and two younger sisters. "I feel like it's really important to be in my family," she says, "because of all the love and stuff. My parents usually cuddle me a lot."

Larkin likes her neighborhood. "It is high on hills and very calm," she says, "and you can see awesome views, and the houses are pretty. I think it's a very pretty place." She also likes that she can get to Haight Street from her house on foot, "if I'm really ready for a walk."

Larkin so loves family life that she and her younger sister play a game called "Sisters." In this game, they do everything they typically do as sisters, but they pretend they are each a year older than they are.

The rules in Larkin's family are no hitting, no punching, no kicking, and no biting. "When I get mad sometimes, I do it by accident," Larkin says.

She wants a family of her own someday, which would include Larkin's husband, three daughters, and one son, who would be the second youngest child. All six would live in the house where Larkin lives now, with her two parents and two sisters. The family of ten would also have a hamster named Poodle.

The combined family would venture out to get ice cream together from the Bi-Rite Creamery near Dolores Park, Larkin says.

Though family is Larkin's highest priority, she also likes seeing friends, and she recently made puppets out of paper bags at a friend's house and put on a puppet show for her friend's family and Larkin's sisters. "It was improv," Larkin explains.

One holiday season, Larkin saw *The Nutcracker* at The San Francisco Ballet. "The Sugar Plum Fairy was my favorite part," she says. "She had a big, fluffy tutu, and she danced around very pretty."

Larkin's favorite family activity is to swim together in her friend's backyard pool or at the Mission Pool, a public pool in San Francisco. She enjoys going with her clan to Grattan Playground, the Ferry Plaza Farmers Market, and the Steinhart Aquarium at the California Academy of Sciences.

"There are jellyfish in there," she says, "and there's a light above them that makes them look like they change colors because they're clear."

Larkin delights in riding her scooter, vacationing in Maine, and going to any movie theater with her family. "I don't have a favorite theater," she says. "I'm OK with what I get. I don't really care where I am, as long as I have my family."

## Insights from the Urban Playground

San Francisco has lots of hills and views. Most San Francisco houses aren't big enough for a family of ten, but families who like to cuddle can always make room.

San Francisco has some house pools, many private pools, and good public pools like the Mission Pool. And on Saturdays, the Ferry Plaza Farmers Market is wonderful for family fun!

Family life in the city can be challenging: San Francisco is an expensive place to live. But as Larkin has discovered, the playgrounds and museums are first rate. It's hard to imagine a place better suited for her beloved family.

# DISCUSSION QUESTIONS

1. What would you add to the "Sisters" game?
2. Would you ever want to combine your current family with your future one? Why or why not?
3. If you put on a paper bag puppet show, what would it be about?
4. What would be fun about swimming in a public pool?
5. If you could see a jellyfish turn any color, what color would you choose?

# Lily, five years old

Five-year-old Lily lives in the Excelsior District with her mom and dad. She does not have any siblings. Lily's cousins live in Colorado and New York, and she misses them very much.

Lily says the funniest person in her family is her cat Ice Cream. Figaro, her other cat, is the one in her family who does nice things for her, like playing with cat toys so Lily can get a few laughs. Lily says she is a good dancer and that her parents love that about her.

Asked what she wishes her parents knew about her, Lily says, "That I have another world that is magical." She has a rich imagination where many characters live, and she plays with them and is good friends with them. Her parents may have some idea about her inner world, Lily says, but they do not know the half of it. She might tell them about it someday, or she might keep it to herself.

Lily loves camping with her family and playing with them at Dolores Park. "I slide on the big slide and go on the swings," she says. Afterward, Lily and her parents get ice cream at Bi-Rite, an ice cream shop right next to the park.

Lily saw the new *Mary Poppins* with her family, and she liked it even better than the first one. She says she often watches movies with her family but never plays sports with them. That's just the kind of family they are, she says.

Lily wants to create her own family one day, and her cousins will be part of it. She will have one daughter, whom she will name Crystal. The family will include a big poodle named Lovey and a furry puppy named Flower. They will live with Lily's grandparents outside of the city "since they have an ocean for swimming," and they will return to San Francisco to visit.

"In my family, we will get to have ice cream whenever we want, and any flavor," she says. "We will dance to hip-hop. And I will not have any sons." In her current family, there are no rules, Lily says. She is allowed to eat ice cream, but not an endless supply like she will allow her family.

One of Lily's friends has two brothers. She also has a big trampoline that people can draw on with chalk, which Lily likes to do. Another friend has one brother and a hot tub that Lily uses. Lily wishes both friends lived with her. "We would play hide-and-seek all the time," she says.

## Insights from the Urban Playground

San Francisco has many hip-hop classes and ice cream shops that await her visits home, along with chalk-bearing trampolines and hot tubs.

San Francisco is a wonderful place to develop the characters in your imagination. If you live here, many fascinating characters walk among you! And the magnificent Opera House can inspire your love for Figaro ... the show, not the cat.

Dolores Park is a wonderful place with a vibrant playground. With Bi-Rite steps away, you don't have to wish for ice cream, though you should leave Ice Cream the cat at home!

**DISCUSSION QUESTIONS**

1. If you were going to name a cat after a food, what name would you choose?
2. Who in your family makes you laugh, and how do they do it?
3. Would you rather watch movies with your family or play sports with them, and why?
4. If you could eat an endless supply of anything, what would it be?
5. What chalk drawing would you create on a trampoline that you could draw on?

# Alex, five years old

~e~

Five-year-old NoPa resident Alex knows the rules in his house: "Don't go under the table during dinnertime," he says. "And no running away from the house without telling my parents. And no talking to strangers. No playing with my parents' phones, and no stealing their money."

Alex lives with his mom, dad, and little sister. Is he good about following his parents' rules? "Not very," he replies.

If Alex could get rid of one of these rules, it would be the one forbidding him from stealing his parents' money. "I already have so much circle money," he says, referring to coins, "and I have zero rectangle money," or dollar bills. He wants more rectangle money.

What would Alex do with rectangle money? "Use it to buy candy and a bigger trampoline," he says. His favorite candies are M&Ms, gummy bears, and cherry sours.

Alex's favorite thing to do with his family is "to ask them questions about how things work," he says. He likes his house "because of all the LEGOs I have and the candies I have," he says, adding that he has over one thousand LEGOs and over one hundred candies.

Alex lives close enough to Golden Gate Park to walk there. "I love to discover things about nature in Golden Gate Park. If you break termites, they can still walk," he explains. "We saw a termite in the park, and we accidentally broke it in half, and we saw it still walking."

As much as he loves his city, Alex does not think he will live in San Francisco as an adult. Why not? "Because it's not very common for people to live where they grew up," he says. He wants to have two kids. "I want them to be funny," he says. "I hope they will be."

When he is an adult, Alex wants to move to Dallas or Singapore. He has been to Dallas to visit his maternal grandmother, and he has never been to Singapore. "I know nothing about Singapore," he says, "except that it's called Singapore. It just sounds like someplace I might want to live."

Wherever he ends up, Alex knows for sure that he wants to live in a city. Alex likes that he can get around easily in a city, "usually taking a bus or a car or walking," he says. "And, most unlikely, a plane."

Asked whether he has been to any small towns, Alex replies, "Japantown," a San Francisco neighborhood. "I've gone to the lobby and seen a movie there," he says. "It was *Ralph Breaks the Internet*."

## Insights from the Urban Playground

Japantown is fun. It is a little section of San Francisco influenced by Japanese culture and filled with Japanese foods, many Japanese people, and a wonderful movie theater, the Kabuki. It's such a unique part of San Francisco that it can feel like its own town.

There's lots of rectangle money in San Francisco, yet many people need more. It is a hard place to live if circle money is all you've got. But for many San Franciscans, the city's features make it worth the expense—Golden Gate Park, for example, where you can learn that broken termites can keep walking.

---

**DiSCUSSiON QUESTiONS**

1. Do you like circle money or rectangle money better, and why?
2. If you could have over one thousand LEGOs or over one hundred candies, which would you prefer?
3. If you saw a broken termite walking, what would you think about that?
4. What do you think living in Singapore would be like?
5. What do you think you would learn if you visited Japantown? Or if you've been there, what did you learn?

# Macy, five years old

~~e~~

Five-year-old Inner Richmond resident Macy admires her older brother. Why? "Because I love him," she says. More specifically? "Because he's being a nice brother."

Macy, who is adopted, has three older brothers, named here as One (the oldest brother), Two (the middle brother), and Three (the youngest brother). Macy is the youngest sibling. Three is the brother Macy named when asked who she looks up to.

With two other brothers to choose from, what makes Three so special? "I don't really know," she answers. She plays with Three the most, but thinks Two is the funniest person in her family. "He makes up jokes, like about a rainbow with wings on it," she says. And he teaches her magic tricks with playing cards.

Macy has a dog: a mix named Smudge. A mix of what, Macy doesn't know, but she knows Smudge was born just before Macy was, but not on the same day.

For her dad's birthday, Macy helped her mom make a peanut-butter-chocolate-caramel cake with M&Ms. Macy's mom has also taught Macy to make scrambled eggs, which Macy can now do without help.

And while the family's house was recently under remodeling construction, Macy and her mom stayed at a hotel across from San Francisco's Museum of Ice Cream. "There was this stuffed unicorn I got," Macy says of the experience, "and there was these candies just hiding on these walls, and I found all of them."

She says the museum smelled like "nothing," and there was a slide leading down into a tub of plastic sprinkles.

Macy also has fun with her dad, shopping at the Ferry Plaza Farmers Market with him on weekends. "We get fruits, and one time I got to have a big piece of watermelon," she says. "There's a whole strawberry person that sells strawberries." At the market, Macy and her dad look at the crabs and lobsters and buy Italian donuts.

Macy lives just a block away from Golden Gate Park. She wants to go to the Conservatory of Flowers, a huge flower garden inside the park. She and her family do a lot of urban hikes, often in the Presidio and in Crissy Field, a former U.S. Army airfield on the water. They have walked across the Golden Gate Bridge a few times, including one Thanksgiving Day.

Macy likes going to the libraries near her home, near her school, and at her school. She likes the book *Serious Farm*. "It's about a farm that has cows and chickens. They all listen to the farm and just copy the farm and be serious," she says.

## *Insights from the Urban Playground*

Walking across the Golden Gate Bridge on Thanksgiving Day! That sounds like a special outing, even for a family who does outdoor activities a lot.

When you have three siblings, attention can be hard to come by, and individual time with a parent can be even more scarce. How lovely that Macy and her dad have the farmers market, and that Macy had the hotel stay and Museum of Ice Cream excursion with her mom.

The Ferry Building is a San Francisco treasure. The Museum of Ice Cream, while a fairly new San Francisco fixture, is a beloved one already!

**DISCUSSION QUESTIONS**

1. What do you think it would be like to be adopted? Or if you are adopted, what is it like for you?
2. What do you think it would be like to have three older brothers? Or if you have three older brothers, what is it like for you?
3. If you could slide into a tub of anything, would you want it to be plastic sprinkles or something else? If something else, what would you want it to be?

4. What would you hope to see the most of if you walked through a huge flower garden in a park, and why?
5. If you could check out any book from the library, would you want it to be about a farm or something else, and why?

# WHAT ARE YOUR
# FAVORITE FOODS?

# Kimaya, seven years old

Seven-year-old Kimaya lives in the Mission with her Papa and Daddy, who are separated. Also living with her are Papa's boyfriend, Victor, and Kimaya's au pair, Erika. Papa's mom spends the night once a week, and Daddy's mom lived with the family half the time for the past two years until she moved into an assisted living facility.

"She's such a cutie," Kimaya says of Erika. Erika, who is from Mexico, taught Kimaya to speak Spanish. Kimaya and Erika speak to each other in Spanish all day. "But sometimes we make expressions in English," Kimaya says, "like 'it's all good in the 'hood.'"

Though her dads live together, Kimaya's Daddy and Papa switch off evenings and weekends with her. Each dad calls his time with Kimaya his "lucky weekend" or "lucky evening."

"I have horseback riding lessons every Saturday," Kimaya says, "and on Daddy's lucky weekends, we go to Boogaloos for brunch on Sunday." Kimaya orders buttermilk pancakes, which she eats along with the tortilla from Daddy's breakfast burrito.

Kimaya also likes waffles, which Papa makes for breakfast. At school, her favorite lunch is "breakfast for lunch—pancakes." Kimaya loves spicy foods, and she eats Wheat Thins with hot sauce.

Kimaya has cerebral palsy, a group of disorders that affects her ability to move and to maintain balance and posture. How does she get around the house? "I crawl," she says, or she walks with help from her family.

When out in the world, Kimaya uses either her walker or a wheelchair, or an adult pushes her in a stroller. "I like playing cards in my stroller," she says. "If I walk all the way to Mission Park using my walker, I get ice cream," she explains. She also takes Lyft sometimes.

Kimaya has three therapists: a physical therapist, "who helps me practice walking on stairs so I won't be afraid," an occupational therapist, "who learns me to take on and off my shirt," and a third therapist, who helps Kimaya with stretches and massage. "I always look forward to therapy because I listen to music in the car on the way there or on the way home," Kimaya says.

Kimaya likes visiting the library and loves to read. "One time, Daddy walked by while I was translating the book *Frog and Toad* into Spanish," she says, adding that Daddy was surprised to hear her translating it while reading. She can also speak in a British accent that she learned from Peppa Pig.

What does Kimaya think about living in San Francisco? "It's great," she says, "because I love Erika."

## Insights from the Urban Playground

You can get around San Francisco easily, whether you walk unassisted or use a walker, wheelchair, or stroller. It's also a good place to use Spanish since there are lots of Spanish speakers in the city, especially in the Mission. If you and your cutie au pair speak Spanish all day, you'll find that many people understand you.

San Francisco foods are as diverse as its families. In the Mission, you can find many spicy foods—lots of spicy foods from Mexico, or if Wheat Thins and hot sauce are your thing, you can find those at your corner store.

1. If you could have a lucky weekend with a parent, what would you want to do together?
2. What would horseback riding be like for you, or if you already do it, how do you like it?
3. Have you ever tried Wheat Thins and hot sauce? If so, did you like it? If not, do you think you would?
4. What do you think would be fun about having three therapists?
5. Can you speak in a British accent, or if you already have one, can you speak in another type of accent?

# Easton, six years old

Six-year-old Easton had pizza at his sixth birthday party, as well as cupcakes he had made. "I had a jumpy castle and forty-seven friends at my house," he says, and a basketball hoop inside the house.

Easton and his ten-year-old sister split their time living between their mom's and dad's houses. He says he used to live in the Mission but moved to the Bayview twelve days ago. His mom said he could go anywhere this weekend. "I really want to go to Spain and France for the weekend," he says.

Though Easton loves pancakes, he usually eats oatmeal for breakfast. Sometimes he starts his day at Craftsman and Wolves in the Mission. "Their eggs are perfect," he says, "and I made some eggs just like them."

Easton prefers home dining to restaurants because he likes to cook and would rather eat "food I cook better than what I can get in a restaurant." He used to take cooking classes, where he learned to make small desserts. He wants to sign up for lessons again.

"I am pretty sure my favorite lunch would be candy," he says. That lunch would be Lucky Charms cereal with chocolate, graham crackers, ice cream, and extra marshmallows in it.

Easton will soon be in first grade. He used to buy lunch from school and liked the burritos. He no longer buys the school lunch because he doesn't know in advance what he'll get, and he doesn't want to be surprised.

He goes to a Chinese summer camp in the Sunset, where he is learning to speak Mandarin. His camp teachers make his lunch, and on Thursdays, he and his campmates get to make s'mores over a grill. They alternate between eating lunch at a campground, a park, and inside a classroom. Easton says there is a brown dog at camp who looks like a baby fox.

Easton's favorite San Francisco dinner spots are all in the Mission: Yamo for chicken noodle soup, Mau for garlic noodles, Supreme Pizza for pepperoni and Hawaiian pizza, and Mixt for salad. "Mixt is across the road from an ice cream place," Easton adds.

What was the last dinner Easton made? "That would be salad and cupcakes," he says. For the salad, he used tomatoes, mushrooms, croutons, and lettuce.

Easton says his mom wants him to eat spicy foods, and his dad does not want him eating Lucky Charms. He prefers mild food to spicy, and sweet foods to salty ones.

Easton's favorite things to do in San Francisco are eating sugar, skimboarding on the ocean, and playing soccer at the park.

## Insights from the Urban Playground

For the kid who likes to prepare their own food, San Francisco has many options: cooking classes, gourmet grocery stores, and dinner prep kits delivered right to their doorstep while they're at school or camp!

Of course, there's lots of sugar here too. Easton may not find Lucky Charms at those fancy food stores, but he can pick up a box at a chain supermarket or most corner markets. And he can get the graham crackers, marshmallows, and chocolate he needs for s'mores at any grocery store. San Francisco has everything he needs to make his perfect, sugary lunch. Yay!

# DiSCUSSiON QUESTiONS

1. Do you get to eat your favorite breakfast food every morning?
2. Do you like to cook your own food or have someone make it for you?
3. Would you like eating candy and sugary cereal for lunch?
4. If you made your own salad, what would you put in it?
5. What kind of foods do you think your parent(s) want you to eat?

# Tessa, five years old

Five-year-old Tessa, a Potrero Hill resident, says pears are her favorite food. Why? "They taste very good, and I have them in my backyard," she says. "I have a plum tree too."

Tessa also likes to watch strawberries grow from her window. "I pick baby strawberries. They taste like babies," she says, laughing.

Her other favorite foods are kale chips, raw carrots, watermelon, oranges, steak, and fish.

When out in the world, Tessa loves to eat macaroni and cheese at The Grove and Swedish princess cake from Woodside's Filoli Garden. She eats chocolate cake on her birthday.

At school, Tessa eats pepperoni pizza and dried mangoes. "I also eat wet mangoes," she says. Dried mangoes make her teeth dry, which gives her cavities, she explains.

Tessa is an only child. She lives with her mom, who adopted her. She says her mom wants her to eat watermelon and drink cranberry juice.

For breakfast, her mom gives her applesauce, peanut butter, fresh fruit, and nuts. For dinner, it's dates wrapped with parmesan cheese and bacon, steak with salsa verde, trout, chicken with yogurt curry lime sauce, pork tenderloin with cherry salsa, or ham with honey mustard.

"Golden brown marshmallows are my favorite for s'mores," Tessa says. She recently made s'mores while camping with her mom and schoolmates at Caswell Memorial State Park. The most fun parts of that trip were eating noodles, grapes, and quesadillas for dinner and swimming in the river.

Tessa says the best place to go in San Francisco is Golden Gate Park, where she climbs structures at the children's playground and feeds the ducks at Stow Lake "because they have that pool," she says of the lake. "That's my really favorite." She also likes playing at Crissy Field.

"I built a city on the beach yesterday," she says, adding that she made it by using driftwood rocks and feathers "from Feather Beach." She says she also climbed a tree.

In addition to s'mores, Tessa's favorite desserts are cashews and grapes, or ice cream—"all flavors," with a sugar cone, she says. "My really best type of ice cream is the swirl," she adds, meaning vanilla and chocolate swirled together. In the fall, she likes making caramel apples by dipping regular apples in liquid caramel and letting it dry.

Tessa likes everything about living in San Francisco, especially taking swim and piano lessons. On the piano, she has learned to play "Hot Cross Buns" and "Twinkle, Twinkle, Little Star." She's eaten both hot cross buns and donuts; asked which she likes better, she answers, "All of them."

## Insights from the Urban Playground

What is better than a park and ice cream? Nothing, and San Francisco has lots of both. The ducks at Golden Gate Park's

Stow Lake are fantastic, and people who visit the lake get to feed them!

Swimming lessons and piano lessons are also wonderful. And camping with your mom and schoolmates? Tessa is lucky to have so many fun life experiences. San Francisco is great for keeping kids busy with exciting adventures, both in the city and nearby.

In San Francisco, you can easily find a lot of healthy food, which it sounds like is mostly what Tessa eats.

---

## DISCUSSION QUESTIONS

1. What do you think baby strawberries taste like?
2. Have you ever eaten dates with parmesan cheese and bacon? If so, do you like them, and if you have not, do you think you would?
3. What materials would you use to make a city on the beach, and what would your city on the beach look like?
4. If you could play a song on the piano that was named after a food, what song would you want it to be?
5. If you could have hot cross buns or donuts, which would you choose, and why?

# Becks, eight years old

Eight-year-old Becks lives in Potrero Hill, home of Goat Hill Pizza, where he orders cheese pizza and spaghetti.

Becks, who lives at home with his mom, dad, and younger twin siblings who are sister and brother, also likes sushi from Moshi Moshi, a sushi bar in the Dogpatch, a neighborhood near Potrero Hill. His usual order there is a soup that has tofu in it and an avocado roll.

But none of these is his favorite food. Becks says the best food is orange chicken from Panda Express. Second best are pupusas, which he gets at school. "But they don't have the sauce I love that I get at home," Becks says.

At four years old, Becks took a cooking class at Bay Leaf Cooking in the Bayview. Bay Leaf no longer exists, so Becks was lucky to learn in its indoor and outdoor kitchens when he did.

"I really want to learn to cook like they do on *Top Chef*," Becks says. He regularly watches the show. "They make desserts using different things, like a black panther out of edible paper."

If Becks could learn to cook anything now, it would be ravioli. "I know my parents like ravioli," he explains. "The first chicken dish I want to learn is chicken tenders because that's easy."

He also wants to learn to make Pokémon and Lego cakes. "I would make a lemon cake of Pikachu. Zekrom would be chocolate," he says. "A Lego cake would be a Lego man looking at you with his hands up. His hat would be vanilla, and his face would be chocolate. His body would be a cookies and cream ice cream cake, with hot chocolate inside."

Becks prefers dining out to eating at home. "At home, I have to make something everyone likes," he explains. His parents also cook. Becks's mom makes chicken noodle soup, and his dad makes pesto pasta.

"I'm excited for my sister and brother to learn to cook," Becks says, "starting with a pizza, then cupcakes, then cookies." They just pretend to cook now, he adds, using a fake oven.

Becks loves living in San Francisco. He plays baseball for the Junior Giants at Oracle Park.

"You get baseball cards every time you show up to practice," he says. "If you get all the cards, then you can get a golden or silver trophy. If you get a golden one, you meet Buster Posey and get a free Giants game ticket."

Becks appreciates his neighborhood. "*Ant-Man and the Wasp* was filmed here," he says of the 2018 superhero film. "And Christopher's Books is the best bookstore."

## Insights from the Urban Playground

A movie filmed in your neighborhood? That would be exciting. It happens in San Francisco a lot. Filmmakers say it is expensive to shoot movie footage in San Francisco, so not every movie team can do it, but many people in San

Francisco have seen film crews in the city if they've lived here long enough.

And the food choices! Not only does San Francisco have Panda Express, which you can find in lots of other places, but also it has Goat Hill and Moshi Moshi, two wonderful restaurants you will only find in San Francisco. Becks has great taste!

---

1. Have you ever been to a sushi bar? If so, what was it like? If not, what do you think it would be like?
2. If you took a cooking class, what is the first thing you'd want to learn to make, and why?
3. What does your parent/do your parents like to eat, and would you like to learn to make it for them?
4. If you met Giants baseball catcher Buster Posey, what would you say to him first?
5. If you could have any movie filmed in your neighborhood, which one would you want to come there, and why?

# J.P., eight years old

Oranges are J.P.'s favorite food. J.P., an eight-year-old Visitacion Valley resident, explains, "They're my favorite color, and they taste good." For the same reasons, J.P. also likes orange chicken, orange-flavored ice cream, grilled cheese sandwiches, mangoes, and cantaloupe.

But don't think you have J.P. all figured out. Even though carrots are orange, J.P. says they are the worst vegetable, whether raw or cooked. He is not a vegetable fan in general, but he says this orange variety is especially terrible.

J.P. loves 7 Mile House, a sports bar and grill in Brisbane. Brisbane is outside of San Francisco, but it's a five-minute drive from J.P.'s house in the city.

J.P. gets ice cream at Polly Ann Ice Cream in the Outer Sunset. He likes that place because he can get the Star Wars flavor, which has orange ice cream mixed into it, among other flavors.

J.P. says the best sports team is the Golden State Warriors, the Bay Area's basketball team. But he also likes going to Giants games at Oracle Park.

One time, J.P. cheered on the Giants while eating multicolored—green, pink, blue, and purple—cotton candy that he and his older brother had sneaked into the ballpark. Their mom and dad didn't know they had it and would have told them they couldn't bring it in or eat it if they had known, J.P. says. They don't like him eating candy or smuggling food.

J.P. is happy he is growing up in the city. He likes walking his dog, Cherokee, to McLaren Park to play basketball with his dad, a San Francisco native. He also rides his bike to Candlestick Point, near the formerly standing Candlestick Park, the stadium where the 49ers football team and the Giants once played.

J.P. likes the beach. On a beach at Candlestick Point, he once rescued three jellyfish on the shore by putting them back in the water. He likes going into the water in his swimsuit, even though San Francisco's bay and ocean water is cold. "I wish San Francisco were warm, like New Jersey," J.P. says.

Once, when J.P.'s maternal grandmother visited from New Jersey, the family took her to Glide Memorial, a church popular with San Franciscans and visitors for its progressive community work, positive messages, and world-class gospel music.

J.P. recently won his school's creativity award for his written biography of Walt Disney, including J.P.'s own drawings. "It's hard for me to talk about the things I do well," he says.

## Insights from the Urban Playground

San Francisco has many orange items for J.P.'s viewing: the Golden Gate Bridge, for instance, or oranges. The city has many parks where J.P. can throw his orange basketball around with his dad.

It's amazing that J.P.'s dad grew up here. It is rare to hear of someone still living in San Francisco who grew up in the city. In recent years, many people have moved away, and even more have moved in. It is now a city of people from everywhere, which means new restaurants and foods to try . . . many of them orange!

---

DISCUSSION QUESTIONS

1. What is your favorite food color?
2. What's the name of your favorite ice cream shop, and why do you like it best?
3. Do you have a parent who was born in the same place you were born?
4. What do you like to do at the beach?
5. If you could give out a creativity award, who would you give it to, and why?

# WHO IS YOUR HERO?

# Alex, eight years old

Eight-year-old Alex's hero is her older sister. To Alex, a hero is someone trustworthy, mostly intelligent, and always there for Alex.

Sometimes Alex and her sister compete over the TV and their dog, Luna, "short for Lunatic." But when she is with her sister, Alex feels protected and safe. Alex says her sister is strong, confident, intelligent, and willing to sacrifice for others.

Does Alex plan on following her sister's example in her own life? "Yes," she says, "except I follow more of an interest in writing, directing movies, writing books, and acting, more than my sister does."

Alex says she could be more like her sister if she became more intelligent, put herself into more acting, thought of comebacks to bullies, grew her hair, and got glasses. She appreciates having her sister to talk to when bad things happen.

Asked whether bad things must happen for heroes to show up, Alex says, "If there are no bad things happening in the world, then the world doesn't exist. There always has to be something bad happening: homeless people, rude people, being broke, having not good eyesight, being mute, blind, deaf. So it's important to actually have problems because otherwise, the earth wouldn't exist since there is always a problem in the world."

Alex is like her hero in some ways. "We both love to sing and act and write. We love doing art, and we both love cats and dogs."

Alex thinks she could be someone else's hero if she "improved on her social interactions." Her friend group had some arguments and stopped playing together for a while, she says, "But then we all got back together, so we weren't broken puzzle pieces anymore."

Alex told one friend to stop being afraid of people who want to go on a date with someone of their same gender. Alex started a detective club at school; the group writes mysteries. She recently ran for president of the club and won.

Alex does not think she is anyone's hero. She believes that if she were a hero, she would have an easier time making friends. Alex thinks it is important to have heroes around and says, "There is a hero in every place, even if it's imaginary." She says heroes are sometimes in a bad mood, and they show it by whining or slamming doors.

Alex loves San Francisco for the variety of foods and smoothies at her favorite bakeries and bagel places. She is also a fan of San Francisco's dog parks, where she and her hero often take their loony dog!

## Insights from the Urban Playground

Sometimes even heroes fight with us over the dog. But if they're good heroes, they also protect us when bullies are nearby or even when our own friends' behavior puzzles us.

They'll join us at dog parks and help us sing, act, and write. And they know people can date anyone of any gender who wants to date the person back. They will back us up on that.

In San Francisco, the many choices for food and smoothies means we have lots of places to go with our heroes. And we might even find out we are secretly their heroes too.

**DISCUSSION QUESTIONS**

1. Who is someone you admire?
2. Why do you look up to this person?
3. Do you plan to follow their example in your own life?
4. Do you think you are like this person?
5. Have you told this person they are your hero?

# *Liam, five years old*

~~~~

Five-year-old Liam, who has lived in San Francisco for just over a year, says, "I've lived in San Francisco for two weeks, but now I'm moving back to Michigan."

Born in Michigan, Liam says he'll miss San Francisco. "Every morning when I wake up," he says, "I smell a delicious smell, and it always smells like San Francisco. I don't know what the smell is, so I can't really tell it to people, but it smells different from ice cream."

Liam, who lives in the Castro, likes the Eureka Valley Dog Park, Oz Pizza on Castro Street, and for ice cream, Castro Fountain or Humphry Slocombe in the Ferry Building.

Asked why he is moving back to Michigan, he replies, "Because my mom wants to move there, and I always agree with my mom."

Liam says a hero is a man that saves a city. "Well, my hero is my daddy, because he's strong and I love him. I know he's a hero because he wears a cape and a yellow-and-black mask." Liam's dad does not save San Francisco, but Liam has seen his dad fight ghost werewolves. "A ghost werewolf is a werewolf that is a ghost," Liam explains.

Another reason Liam's dad is his hero? He is funny, Liam says. Asked whether his dad tells jokes, Liam replies, "Well, dad jokes." His dad also launches tickle missiles, which is when his hand starts "up in the air," then lands on Liam's stomach, forehead, cheeks, and legs, tickling the landing spot.

On further reflection, Liam says his dad does save the city after all. "Well, he kind of saves everybody else in my family too," Liam adds, referring to his mom, his little sister, and him. But his dad is retiring from being a hero. "Now he's a spine surgeon," Liam says.

Maybe Liam's dad saves only his own family now. "Well, my dad doesn't save my sister very much because she's pretty strong. She can save herself from a werewolf." He has not seen his sister do this because she fights werewolves at night, when Liam is asleep. His mom is also strong, Liam says, "so she can even save herself from a giant."

Does this mean Liam's dad saves only Liam? "I'm pretty good on my own too," Liam says. "I don't fight with werewolves or giants. I fight bad people. I'm only stronger than people." He fights people by sitting on them until they turn into dust.

Liam used to save the entire city, but no longer. "I'm not that guy anymore," he says.

## Insights from the Urban Playground

San Francisco is the right place for fighting werewolves, giants, and bad people. Loaded up on Castro Fountain or Humphry Slocombe ice cream, you can stay awake all night to save the city.

According to Liam, the city also smells fantastic, at least in the morning. The city has both spine surgeons and heroes, even if it is losing a spine surgeon and three heroes—since Liam is not that guy anymore—when Liam and his family move to Michigan.

When you're in San Francisco, beware of tickle missiles! Liam's dad may not be the only person in the city launching them.

---

1. What does it smell like in the morning where you live?
2. What ice cream flavor do you think heroes like the best?
3. Do you always agree with your parent(s)?
4. Do you know anyone strong enough to fight ghost werewolves, giants, or bad people?
5. Do you think heroes always turn into spine surgeons when they retire, or can they become something else?

# Willa, nine years old

Nine-year-old Willa lives in Bernal Heights with her mom and dad. She doesn't have any siblings. Willa admires Ava, the daughter of someone Willa's mom knows.

"Ava is in college. I think people that are older than me are wiser than me," Willa says. "Ava is my hero because some people are just full of themselves when you're around them, but Ava acknowledges everyone in the room," Willa says.

"I'm a little bit full of myself sometimes, and I'm hoping to not be full of myself," she admits.

"I hosted a sleepover with a friend, and she is easygoing, and I took that to my advantage. Let's say there is a vanilla cupcake and a red velvet cupcake, and the friend says she doesn't care, but she wants the red velvet cupcake. So I say, 'I'll have the red velvet one,' and I see her face droop, but she's like, 'OK, I'll have the vanilla.' You can see I took advantage of her."

It is different with Ava. "She's easygoing too," Willa says, "but no one takes advantage of her because she's so easygoing that people are like, 'I better cherish that.'"

Willa says people who help others are also heroes, like her mom, who helps her with her homework.

Willa has been a hero. "Once I had on this pretty white dress," she says. "We had a garden party, and my grandma unboned the steak and put a plate of steak on a picnic bench. My dog started to chew a piece. I thought there were bones in the steak and worried that they could get caught in his very small neck. So I get down on the grass, and I stick my hand in his mouth, and a few minutes later, I have to change because there's lots of swallowed meat on my dress."

Willa says it's important for the world to have heroes. "Or else the world wouldn't be what it is," she says. "They're not superheroes like '*da-na-na-na-na-na-na-na*'"—(singing the *Batman* song)—"they're different kinds of heroes. I think the world is stable, but without those little deeds being done every day, maybe something wouldn't be here, like my dog wouldn't be here."

Willa loves living in San Francisco because all her immediate neighbors' backyards are connected to hers, without fences. These neighbors have kids, so she can easily play with her friends.

"San Francisco is diverse," she adds, "and if it was medieval times, and San Francisco was a city with walls, we could survive. We have everything we need in this city."

## Insights from the Urban Playground

San Francisco can be a fun place for kids, especially in neighborhoods where there are lots of kids the same age with connected backyards. Communal yards are not common in the city, so Willa has something special.

What fun to have a college-age person to look up to! Especially one who isn't full of herself and who acknowledges everyone in the room. Admirable, indeed!

We may be in modern times, but it's nice to know there is enough in the city to ensure survival in medieval conditions. Knowing there's enough to go around can help all San Franciscans be easygoing!

---

1. Can you think of a time when you took advantage of a friend? If so, what happened?
2. Do you think a parent helping a child with homework is heroic? Why or why not?
3. What would you do if you thought a dog were choking on a bone?
4. What would be the best part about having a backyard connected to your neighbors' backyards?
5. What would be hard about living in a city in medieval times?

# Cal, nine years old

Nine-year-old Cal admires his dad. "He is creative, and he's the owner of a workplace," Cal says. Cal also looks up to his dad's employees for their creativity.

"I am kind of creative too, when I play football," Cal adds. He is a wide receiver and a leader on his team, and he makes creative plays. Cal doesn't plan to be a business owner like his dad. Instead, he wants to be a wide receiver in the NFL. He looks up to Green Bay Packers quarterback Aaron Rodgers, but the Oakland Raiders are Cal's favorite team.

Cal says his real hero is his mom. She does everything for Cal, like making him his favorite food, penne with butter. She also drives him to his friends' houses and his football and baseball games. Cal feels happy when he is with her.

According to Cal, a hero is kind and nice, like his mom. They also help people like she does. "Everyone can be a hero because everyone is nice," he says.

Anyone can help someone if they fall or teach someone something they don't know how to do. Cal is heroic when he plays with people at school who would not have anyone to play with otherwise.

To be someone else's hero, Cal would teach them how to throw a football. His favorite place in San Francisco is his backyard, where he plays football with his mom and dad. He could also share food with people who don't have any food and throw a fundraiser to buy homeless people homes.

"I could also plant plants in a grassy field, like Crissy Field," Cal says, referring to a former US Army airfield where people in San Francisco have picnics and run along the water.

He thinks the hardest part of being a hero would be having to do it all the time. "It would be nice to have a break," he says.

In fact, the best part about being a hero would be teaching others to be nice, to spread the heroism around, Cal says.

Cal believes heroes have bad moods sometimes. "They wouldn't show anyone, but they feel it on the inside," he explains. "They're human."

Cal says there are heroes everywhere in the world, and they all speak differently from each other and do different things. For example, he says, a hero in New York stops crime.

When Cal thinks of heroes, superheroes come to mind. His favorite superhero is Spiderman. "He can shoot webs. It's cool. And he's kind and nice, and he helps people," Cal says.

## *Insights from the Urban Playground*

San Francisco has many heroes sharing their food with those who need it and helping people who don't have homes to get them. It's a good way to be a hero in the city. San Francisco needs creative people like Cal to help figure out how to feed and house people.

Kindness and niceness are important in San Francisco. People in this city might not always show how sad they are when other San Franciscans don't have food to eat or a place to live, but most everyone wishes they could be a hero to someone who is in need.

---

DISCUSSION QUESTIONS

1. If being a hero means teaching someone to do something they don't know how to do, what could you teach someone?
2. If you could throw a fundraiser for any group of people, who would it be?
3. What do you think the hardest part about being a hero would be?
4. Do you think heroes are ever in a bad mood?
5. Who is your favorite superhero, and why?

# Auggie, nine years old

Nine-year-old Auggie admires his mom. She is one of his heroes because she's a prekindergarten teacher and a mom, and she is adventurous.

"She likes to hike," Auggie says. "She hikes around the Presidio, and she is brave because she will not take down a challenge."

Auggie does not like to hike, but he enjoys riding his bike in the Presidio, a San Francisco park with lots of trees and trails. He also likes selling lemonade and cookies with his sister, at $1 per item, when they set up a lemonade stand in front of their house in their NoPa neighborhood. They have earned as much as $22.

Auggie's mom is heroic "when she's able to keep her cool while dealing with a bunch of crazy five-year-olds," Auggie says, meaning his mom's prekindergarten students. Auggie has never seen his mom teach, but his mom tells stories about her job, calling them "funnies of the day."

Auggie says his mom's students probably think she is a good teacher: "one who never backs down from a challenge, is always there for her students, and is proud to be a teacher."

World wrestling champion John Cena is also Auggie's hero. "He's really strong, and he has abs," Auggie says. Asked whether he wants abs of his own, Auggie replies, "I mostly want just muscle, but I guess also abs."

John Cena acts heroic all the time, Auggie says. "He never backs down to wrestle somebody. Even if he gets defeated, he's not scared; he just tries again. When he's in the ring wrestling, even if he's not feeling well and he's hurt, he's still going to try to pin the other person."

To be more like John Cena, Auggie says, he could do some push-ups to stay in shape, do well in school, exercise a lot, eat many sources of protein, and try not to eat too much sugar.

Auggie says San Francisco comic book author Judd Winick writes heroes into his book series, *Hilo*. "Hilo will go to the end of the earth to save his sister or his friend D.J.," Auggie says. Auggie has read all of the published *Hilo* books.

Auggie believes he is a hero to his dog, Didi, because he feeds her sometimes. He says he doesn't think he is anyone else's hero because he can't stand up to a bully.

What could make him heroic? "Doing something I've never done, like a frontflip or a backflip off something bouncy, like a trampoline," he says. Auggie doesn't take gymnastics lessons yet, but he wants to.

## Insights from the Urban Playground

For anyone seeking hero status by Auggie's definition, there are lots of adventures to try in San Francisco. There are many hiking and biking trails, not just in the Presidio but all over the city.

You can go to a bookstore for a *Hilo* reading and meet Judd Winick. You can even go to House of Air, a place with lots of trampolines, and try a front- or backflip with Auggie.

Like Auggie and his sister, you can have a lemonade and cookie stand too! San Francisco is bustling like all urban centers, but some neighborhoods, like Auggie's, feel residential.

**DISCUSSION QUESTIONS**

1. What does the word "hero" mean to you?
2. Does your teacher keep their cool while teaching you and your classmates?
3. What is one adventure you would like to try, a challenge from which you would not back down?
4. Do you think book authors are heroes?
5. Do you think you are a hero to any animals?

# WHAT IS YOUR
# FAVORITE HOLIDAY?

# Eliza, six years old

Christmas is six-year-old Eliza's favorite holiday. "I like all the presents," she says. "My favorite Christmas present was this Play-Doh I can make a sandwich with." She decorates her house with different colored lights and puts a star on top of the Christmas tree.

Eliza celebrates the holiday with "my grandma, my auntie, my cousin, my little brother, my little sister, my mom, my other auntie, and my other cousin." All these people except one aunt and one cousin live with Eliza in her house in Visitacion Valley.

This Christmas, Eliza might get a new hairspray for her mom, a baby toy for her little sister, and a toy dinosaur for her little brother.

She also goes to her dad's house in South San Francisco on Christmas. "Last Christmas," she says, "I made a paper snowman and taped it on my dad's door. He loved it."

About San Francisco, Eliza says, "It's fine. I like the flowers," red and pink roses being her favorite. She also likes the city's birds. "I like talking to them," she says. "I say 'tweet, tweet, tweet, tweet' to them."

Eliza's favorite bird is a pigeon. "I like that I can catch them," she says. "And they are so fun to play with. I named one Ella."

A holiday Eliza doesn't like is Halloween. "It scares me," she says. "I saw some decoration ghosts on the tree, and it scared me." She ventures out to get candy, saying, "I have fun with the treats."

Last Halloween, she dressed as Fancy Nancy. "It looked like Fancy Nancy because it was just because of my hair," she says, explaining that her hair was curly and sticking up.

If Eliza could invent a holiday, she would call it "Cotton Candy Rain." "Cotton candy would fall out of the sky," she says. "I would run and catch it and make it go on my hair, and so I don't have to get a snack. I just eat my hair." The holiday would take place every day of the year, and people would sing a song called "Cotton Candy Rain" one hundred times a day.

Eliza's favorite San Francisco activity is to "go in the car, to go to a tea party." She likes the Crown & Crumpet Tea Stop Café on the border of Japantown and Lower Pacific Heights.

Eliza also likes to dance ballet, which she does every Saturday in Daly City, ten minutes south by car from San Francisco's southern tip. Her favorite step is spring points. "I like about it that you point your toes," she says.

## Insights from the Urban Playground

San Francisco does get some scary decorations on Halloween! But there are some beautiful ones at Christmas. So many lights on all the houses! And you'll even see decoration snowpeople, Santa, Rudolph the Red-Nosed Reindeer, and many other exciting images.

Fancy Nancy would probably like San Francisco since you can have crazy, messy hair in the city whenever you want. No one's really going to notice, or if they do, they won't say anything. Chances are, their hair is wild too!

San Francisco has some great tea houses for tea parties. It's a marvelous place to be a little kid!

## DISCUSSION QUESTIONS

1. What are your favorite Christmas decorations, and why?
2. What is your favorite type of flower?
3. Do you talk to birds, and if so, do you tweet at them or say something else?
4. Do you think Fancy Nancy likes Halloween? Why or why not?
5. Can you make up and sing the "Cotton Candy Rain" song?

# Duncan, five years old

Five-year-old Duncan, an only child, lives in Pacific Heights with his mom and the Mission with his dad. "That's my normal family," he says, "and then I have other parts of my family: my Harmony and Grandpa, my Nana and Papa."

Just before Christmas, Duncan's favorite holiday, he and his mom visit Duncan's maternal grandfathers, Harmony and Grandpa, in San Mateo. "Their real names are Mark and Shane," he says. "The day after Christmas, I go with my dad to Oregon for five days to see my other grandparents, Nana and Papa. Two Christmases for me!"

Duncan has big plans for his next birthday, three months away. "I'm going to have a ghost owl party," he says. "A ghost owl is an owl with a black crown and five jewels who can turn into a ghost."

"The party will have a ghost owl cake. It's going to have my family and nobody else. I'm going to have a radio that can play music, and we will have a dance party, and we're going to have a special lunch. I haven't planned all of it yet."

Duncan says he learned about ghost owls in a movie. "I cannot tell you what happens in the movie," he says. "It's pretty violent."

Duncan's second favorite holiday after Christmas is Easter. Why? "I search for a ghost owl chocolate egg at my mom's house," he says. "When you break it open, there's a ghost inside."

If Duncan could invent a holiday, it would be called "The Holiday of the Big Tree." It would take place in the twenty-second month of the year and would last for twenty-five years.

"There's a ginormous tree full with ornaments that's one thousand feet high," he explains. "At the top, there is a star, and when it breaks open, fireworks launch out of it." The tree is ten blocks from either his mom or his dad's house, whichever one Duncan is at when the holiday comes around.

"In Japan, they call this holiday 'The Tree Star,'" Duncan says. "In Italy, they have ten trees that are ten feet high, and six stars in the center, and one ginormous star in the middle of the six stars. Almost everybody in Italy comes to see the tree."

Duncan's favorite thing about San Francisco is the Golden Gate Bridge. "Once, I was driving across the bridge and I saw a lot of people walking across it," he says. How many? "I would say about 112. By the way, there's other famous bridges, and they're not as famous as the Golden Gate."

## Insights from the Urban Playground

Ghost owls sound like quite something! There could be lots of them in San Francisco. The city is so bustling and busy, you could miss seeing an owl with a crown and jewels, especially if it turned into a ghost.

It's a good city for a holiday with big trees. There are forests all over the city, or the Big Tree could stand alone in one of San Francisco's many parks.

The Golden Gate Bridge is wonderful, and there are often 112 people walking on it . . . sometimes more! And like Duncan says, many other bridges are not as famous.

# DISCUSSION QUESTIONS

1. If you could ask a ghost owl one question, what would it be?
2. If you found a ghost inside a chocolate egg, what would you do?
3. On The Holiday of the Big Tree/The Tree Star, what would be your favorite ornament to see, and why?
4. Would you prefer to celebrate The Holiday of the Big Tree/The Tree Star in San Francisco, Japan, Italy, or somewhere else?
5. Would you rather walk or drive across the Golden Gate Bridge?

# Khylee, seven years old

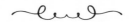

Christmas is seven-year-old Khylee's favorite holiday because "you get a lot of presents, and you spend time with your family." Khylee lives close to Ingleside Heights, and she has family in the city and the greater Bay Area, as far out as Brentwood.

"I usually eat my family's two food countries," Khylee adds. Her family is Spanish and Chinese. She says that for the Spanish side, she eats mashed potatoes, and for the Chinese side, she eats rice with soy sauce and soup.

Sometimes Khylee celebrates Christmas at her house and sometimes at her aunt and uncle's house. "We also go to a fun trip," she says, like Disneyland.

To prepare for Christmas, Khylee wraps presents and "sets up the tree," placing ornaments on it and a star on top. She says her mom works the hardest to prepare for Christmas, then her dad, who helps Khylee decorate the tree. Both parents watch her baby brother while getting ready for the big day.

"My brother relaxes the most on Christmas," she says. "We went to my auntie and uncle's house last Christmas, and everybody carried him."

The best Christmas gift Khylee has given someone is a basketball for her cousin and a Minnie Mouse dress for her other cousin.

The only holiday Khylee doesn't like is Halloween "because it's about scary stuff, and I don't like scary stuff," she says. She finds it scary when people dress as zombies; she prefers to dress as a princess. Last year, she was Tiana, and she was Cinderella the year before that.

Khylee does like trick-or-treating. "I go with my auntie," she adds, and says she wishes she could stay out collecting candy until 9:00 p.m.

Khylee's baby brother went out trick-or-treating last Halloween, when he also relaxed more than everyone else, with Dad pushing him in a stroller. Khylee says her brother was dressed up as baby Jack-Jack from *The Incredibles*, even though he didn't know it was Halloween.

Khylee's dad likes Halloween, so he always decorates the house. Khylee says her dad wanted to go out as a zombie last year, but he got so busy setting up the house that he ran out of time to dress up. This was just fine with her!

For this Halloween, Khylee wants her family to dress up together on a theme, like Winnie the Pooh.

Speaking of coordinated outfits, if Khylee could invent a holiday, she would make it a three-day event called "Family Time," where families wear matching pajamas. They would also cook a family recipe and sing together.

## Insights from the Urban Playground

Being close to Disneyland is a wonderful part of San Francisco life. You can go there for the holidays or even a long weekend.

People in the city come from different backgrounds, including Spanish and Chinese. If you visited Khylee's home at Christmas, you could eat food from a family recipe. You could also see her baby brother relaxing while everyone prepares for the special day.

On Halloween, you could help Khylee's dad stage the house for trick-or-treaters, though you might save him time that he could use to assemble his zombie costume, which would not make Khylee very happy!

**DiSCUSSiON QUESTiONS**

1. Do you eat food from any family recipes on holidays?
2. Do you ever decorate a tree or your home on holidays?
3. Who in your family relaxes the most on holidays, and how do you know they are the most relaxed?
4. Do any Halloween costumes scare you?
5. What would you think of a holiday where your family members wore matching outfits?

# Courage, seven years old

Seven-year-old Courage likes Halloween. "It's scary and gruesome," he says.

"I don't dress up as anything scary," Courage adds. "I do something creative." One year, he dressed up as a blue dragon, using costume materials he'd picked out at Party City at Serramonte Center, a mall just south of his city of San Francisco.

His family is vegan and his dad doesn't let him eat candy, so Courage does Halloween at his grandparents' home, also in San Francisco. Gummy bears, Snickers, and Kit Kats are Courage's favorite candy. The worst thing someone could give him when he trick-or-treats? Carrots.

Every year, Grandpa puts together his flaming pumpkin: He sets a jack-o'-lantern over a hole in his outdoor wooden work table, precut for just this purpose. When a trick-or-treater takes too much candy, Grandpa pulls an air compressor from inside the house, and fire comes from the bottom of the pumpkin out of the top of its head. Courage loves that trick.

Courage does not like Easter because "I don't like walking everywhere, and I don't like backtracking," he says, referring to Easter egg hunts.

If Courage could invent a holiday, he would make one up called "Skillszot." Skillszot is a two-night holiday where people do not have school the day between the two nights, and they can do whatever they want.

On the two nights of Skillszot, family members and friends gather around a fire in the middle of the street. Courage's group would meet outside his grandparents' house. Wherever people celebrate Skillszot, everyone goes around the circle, and one by one, each person shows off one special skill over the fire.

"For example," Courage says, "They would do a cartwheel in the air, over the fire . . . or a backflip."

This repeats ten times. If you don't have ten skills, or even one, no problem. "It's skippable," Courage says. But even those who feel short on talent can skip school for Skillszot.

There would be "really crazy" music, and everyone would have dinner at 9:00 p.m. There would be no clapping and no competition, but lots of foam pads to protect people who fall and a bridge over the fire, so no one could get burned. There would be no singing or dressing up. Everyone would drink Gatorade.

Which of Courage's ten skills would he put on display for Skillszot? "I don't really have ten skills," he says. But he's got a few. For one, he can run fast while leaning far to the side. He can also walk like a crab and hold his own in a light saber battle.

## Insights from the Urban Playground

In San Francisco, Skillszot could work. In many neighborhoods, you can't easily drive a car down the street because there are so many other cars on it, and the sidewalks are jammed with people.

But in lots of neighborhoods, you can have block parties, garage sales, and special gatherings like Skillszot. You can trick-or-treat through neighborhoods, although many groups travel in packs. But you can go with just your family to any door you choose, as long as there's someone there to give you candy or someone has left some for you. Just don't take too much from Courage's grandpa!

---

1. What is your favorite holiday?
2. What are your three favorite types of candy?
3. Do you play any tricks on Halloween?
4. If you could invent a holiday, what would it be?
5. What ten skills would you display at Skillszot?

# Desi, nine years old

~~~~

Nine-year-old Desi, an only child, lives in Crocker-Amazon with his mom and the Outer Sunset with his dad. He is in a Mandarin immersion program at school, and he likes taking tennis lessons and flying his drones in Golden Gate Park.

Desi's favorite holidays are Christmas and Halloween. For Christmas, he and his mom drive to Santa Barbara to celebrate with his family on his mom's side: his aunts, uncles, grandparents, and great-grandparents.

Desi's family exchanges gifts through a White Elephant game. Everyone brings one wrapped gift. Each person either pulls a wrapped gift from the pile or takes an unwrapped one from its previous owner. Desi's top winnings were a mini Lego set and an electric toothbrush.

On Halloween, Desi trick-or-treats in the Mission. "One house serves brains and eyeballs in cups," he says, referring to Jell-O made to look like these body parts.

Last year, he dressed up as pink cotton candy. He and his mom made the costume out of pink mesh screen door material. "Everyone thought I was a unicorn," he says, because they mistook the crown on his head for a unicorn's horn. This year, Desi plans to go as either a cardboard box, an alien, or a robot.

After trick-or-treating, Desi stays up and organizes his candy by type—"Milky Way with Milky Way, lollipops with lollipops," he says. For his mom and his aunt, he sets aside his Kit Kats, their favorite.

Another holiday Desi loves is Pride. On July 4, he went to a parade in Marin that he thought was a Pride Parade. He remembers the day as fun and warm, even though a bee stung him underfoot when he had his shoes off.

"I put ice on the sting, and here I am now," he says. "A bee sting is like a mosquito bite, except more painful."

If Desi could invent a holiday, it would be "Yipee," the word people would say while running through the streets in their pajamas on a Tuesday and Wednesday every January. They would say that because they would leave school or work early on Tuesday, then go back late on Wednesday.

On Yipee, everyone would walk across a peppermint bridge, over a sea of candy, at an imaginary San Francisco spot called "Holiday Island." They could pull candy from the sea. "The candy keeps generating," Desi explains. "You take it home, eat it, and get cavities."

Wednesday at noon, the candy bridge would fall down, turn into stone, and crumble into the ocean. The candy would turn into fish, and sharks would eat it.

### *Insights from the Urban Playground*

San Francisco is a fun place to be a kid. Brains and eyeballs! Flying drones in the park! And a peppermint bridge with unlimited candy underneath, if Desi gets his wish.

Even the holidays that already exist are great. In San Francisco, kids often trick-or-treat in groups, on streets in certain neighborhoods, like Desi's spot in the Mission.

The city has all kinds of schools where kids can focus on learning languages other than English—like Mandarin at Desi's school, or French or Italian.

Not every holiday is Pride Weekend, but in San Francisco, it can feel like Pride every day.

---

DiSCUSSiON QUESTiONS

1. What would you do if you saw a drone flying above you in the park?
2. If you were part of a White Elephant gift exchange, do you think you would take your chances with a wrapped present or take something already unwrapped from someone else?
3. If you were going to be pink cotton candy for Halloween one year, how would you make your costume?

4. What is the best part of a Pride Parade? If you haven't been to one, what do you think would be the best part

5. If you could pull something from an unlimited sea of candy for one day, what would you go for first?

# WHO ARE YOUR PETS?

# Nicolas, nine years old

Lower Haight resident Nicolas, nine years old, has approximately 1,002 pets: two parakeets and one thousand bees.

Buddy and Rocky are the parakeets. They are not siblings. Buddy is a year old and has been in Nicolas's family for a few months. He is white in some places, with a light blue belly, and has black dots on his blue wings. When he is not in his cage, he flies around the house. He does not chirp much.

"Buddy likes to be with his friend," Nicolas says of Rocky, the family's other bird, who is younger than Buddy and has been in the family for just a few weeks. "They're always together."

According to Nicolas, Rocky chirps a lot. Like Buddy, Rocky has a blue belly. He also has black crooked stripes on his back, which is also green. "He has little cheeks with black dots," Nicolas adds.

Though Buddy and Rocky like each other, they have their fights. "Sometimes when they want a place to sleep," Nicolas says, "they peck at each other and squawk a lot."

Nicolas's family feeds the birds seeds and millet, which they buy from The Animal Company on Castro Street, a store that sells birds and bird-related supplies. "They like millet a lot because it's like their candy," Nicolas explains.

What is the best part of having birds? "They're really fun to play with, and I like them," Nicolas says. "They're really cute. I make tunnels for them by holding up blankets over them, and they walk through. And sometimes they play in their water dish."

The most surprising thing about having birds is when Nicolas talks to them and they answer. Buddy and Rocky have said "Good morning," "Hi," and "Hello" to Nicolas. "I tried to teach them 'My name is Buddy,' and 'My name is Rocky," Nicolas says, "but they never really answered."

Asked whether he wishes he were like the birds in any way, Nicolas answers, "I wish I could fly. Then I could see on top of everything, what's going on. I would get to soar through the air."

As for the bees, the family keeps the hive in the backyard. None of their roughly one thousand bees have names, but Nicolas thinks they like being part of his family. "They like the sun, where we keep them," he explains.

"It's fun to watch them go in and out of the hive with their pollen pants," he adds, referring to sacks of pollen they have on their legs. "Also, they make their own honey, which we get to eat."

## Insights from the Urban Playground

San Francisco has good beehive weather. There's not much rain, it never snows, and it is rarely too cold or hot by a bee's standards. The same goes for birds, but you can keep those inside, anyway, like Nicolas's family does.

In quirky San Francisco, of course there's a store devoted to birds. And there is a lot of millet because many people in the city like it too . . . but maybe not for dessert!

If Nicolas could fly like his family's bees and birds do, he would have a spectacular view of a magnificent city. Imagine everything he could see!

---

1. If you could have one thousand bees and two parakeets or one thousand parakeets and two bees, which would you want, and why?
2. If you had a bird with many colors, what colors would it be, and in what spots?
3. If you could teach birds to say anything, what words would you teach them?
4. If you could fly, what place would you fly over to see it from above, and why?
5. If you had one thousand bees, would you name them, and if so, what are some of the names you would give them?

# Mia, seven years old

Seven-year-old Mia just moved to Oakland after living her entire life on Treasure Island in San Francisco.

Mia lives with her mom, dad, big sister, little brother, dog, and two betta fish. Her dog is a pit bull named Ace, and Ace has been in Mia's family since before she was born.

"He has white all down his nose and in his paws, and his feet are white, and the rest is brownish and blackish," Mia says. Ace knows Mia when he sees her, Mia says. She can tell because "he just wags his tail and comes to me."

Ace likes baths, Mia says. She knows because he took a bath once and "he was so chillaxed." Mia's favorite thing to do with Ace? "Well, I used to snuggle with him at night," she says.

Mia isn't sure why Ace does not snuggle with her anymore, but she has a stuffy to snuggle with now, a puppy named Puppy. Mia prefers to snuggle with stuffies over real animals "because stuffies are very snuggly."

Mia says Ace likes being part of her family. She can tell "because he's very happy when he sees his family . . . and his mom is still alive." Mia says Ace's mom lives with Mia's cousin Julie.

What are the names of Mia's two betta fish? "I don't know," she says. "One is all blue, and one is like pinkish or reddish, and then there was white," she says.

The betta fish do not live together because they are fighting fish, Mia explains. The blue one lives in a tank. Asked what its personality is like, Mia says, "He just swims, and sometimes we give him food." The pink, red, and white one lives in a bowl. What is its personality? "He just swims and swims," Mia says. Mia's dad cleans the tank and the bowl.

What do the fish eat? "Well, I don't know what the one that's white, red, and pink eats," Mia says. "And then the other one, the blue fish, eats three little balls of fish food."

Mia used to have guinea pigs and wants another "because they're so cute. They liked to cuddle with my grandpa," she says.

If Mia could have any pet she has never had, she would want a panda. "I will snuggle with her every night," she says. Mia's panda would be purple, and she would eat bamboo. Mia would name her The Purpliest Panda.

"When she's born, she would be zero," Mia says, "but when she gets older, she's going to be up to one thousand."

## Insights from the Urban Playground

Treasure Island is fascinating. It's an artificial island that is part of San Francisco City and County, but you have to drive or take a bus there from the main part of the city. It's rare to meet someone who grew up on Treasure Island, since only 2,500 people live there.

Treasure Island would be a wonderful place to raise a dog since it's so quiet. You and your dog, or your stuffed dog, can snuggle in peace!

Treasure Island may be small, but it's large enough to hold two fighting fish in separate spaces . . . and two parents and their three kids.

1. How would you like living on an island that is part of a city?
2. Do you like snuggling with real animals or stuffed animals better, and why?
3. Would it be good to have a pet whose mom lived with your cousin? Why or why not?
4. If you could have a pet you have never had, what type of animal would you choose, and why?
5. If you could have a pet in your favorite color, what color would your pet be?

# Elliott, seven years old

"I have a brother named Wally," says Elliott, a seven-year-old only child in Duboce Triangle. "He is a golden retriever, half goldendoodle. And he's a very good dog."

Wally has lived with Elliott and his two dads for eight months. Elliott loves to throw Wally a ball at a park within walking distance of their house.

What is Wally's personality like? "Sometimes he bites, and most of the time, he's laying down," Elliott says. When Wally sees people and dogs he doesn't know, he smells them.

Wally only barks when Elliott and his dads are going to the car. "He doesn't want us to leave," Elliott explains.

Elliott taught Wally to walk downstairs, wake Elliott up, give people a pawshake, and sit. "Now he's in the chewing stage. My dad's shoe broke," Elliott says, referring to a time when Wally was home alone. "Right now, I learned him to do a piggyback ride, but only two legs on my back."

Elliott once dressed Wally up in one of Elliott's costumes, a cape. "He took it off hisself with his teeth," Elliott adds.

Elliott received Wally as a gift for his seventh birthday. He and his dads were celebrating Elliott's birthday in St. Louis with Elliott's cousins. Elliott had been asking for a dog.

"We drive there, and I didn't even know I was getting a dog," Elliott says. "It was my birthday day, so we were going to so many places to get all the stuff. But they tricked me," he said of his dads' surprise gift.

Elliott's family has a house in Sonoma, with a pool where Elliott's dad taught him to swim at four years old. Wally goes to Sonoma with the family, but he does not swim. How does Wally like the road trip? "He's fine with it," Elliott says. "He just lays down."

Elliott likes his life in San Francisco. "I like many things," he says. "I like the Golden Gate Bridge; I like life." His favorite school activity is knitting, and he recently knitted a flute case that he can carry around his neck. Does Elliott play the flute? "Uh, not really," he answers, but he wants to learn.

"I also made a ball and a gold, orange, and white chicken." He's going to knit something for Wally. "Maybe a hat," Elliott says. "He's good with hats."

Elliott once had a fish that he named Window. What inspired the name? "I think I just saw a window," he says. Elliott wants a pet monkey, whom he would name Branch, since the monkey would climb branches.

## Insights from the Urban Playground

Many San Franciscans have second houses with pools in the country. Sonoma is a little over two hours north of San Francisco by car—not too bad for a dog. And Sonoma has so much land for a dog to run around in. What a nice life Wally has!

The city is good for dogs, too, since San Francisco has many parks. Elliott and Wally are two lucky brothers, being able to walk to a park from their house! Adding a monkey to the family could be challenging since San Francisco isn't really set up for monkeys, except at the zoo.

---

# DISCUSSION QUESTIONS

1. If you met Wally, what would you say to him while shaking his paw?
2. If you had a dog who ate your family's shoes when you left the house, how would you train the dog to stop?
3. If you could receive a knitted gift, would you prefer a ball, a chicken, or a flute bag?
4. What kind of hat would you put on Wally's head if you had the chance?
5. If you could name a fish after anything you saw, would you name it Window or something else, and why?

# Sara, nine years old

Sara, a nine-year-old girl in Noe Valley, does not always sleep through the night. Her younger brother and roommate wakes her up to go to his parents' room. Her brother has a blanket that falls from his bed every night, which also wakes Sara up. "I'm a sensitive sleeper," Sara explains.

What does Sara's little brother like best about her? "The fact that I share with him, even though he doesn't share with me," she says.

Sara's favorite thing to do in San Francisco is "probably go out to the park or watch a family movie on Friday, maybe have dinner and chat," she says.

Asked what she wishes her family knew about her, Sara answers, "They probably don't know that the loss of our old dog hurts me way more than it hurts them."

The family dog, Shadow, ran outside when Sara left the front door open. Strangers took Shadow in and accidentally fed her something she wasn't supposed to eat, which made her die. Sara says lots of people explained to her that it's not her fault, but she still blames herself.

Sara, who has "three boy cousins, one girl cousin," and her little brother, wants a family of her own someday. She would have two daughters and "a million pets": a dog, a guinea pig, horses, parrots, hamsters, and several fish.

Sara's family has a rule that on Saturday morning, no one can go straight to the TV after waking up; her mom, her dad, and her little brother must say good morning to each other before they can watch TV.

Sara says Sierra, the new family dog, was meant for her family. When they went to the puppy place to pick out their new dog, Sara chose Sierra of the two eligible puppies. "She ran up to me and kissed me," Sara says. "The other puppy just started, I don't know, climbing me."

When Sierra was a puppy, Sara's family kept her in a pen inside their house. "Well, goldendoodles are known to be really smart," Sara says. "We have a camera at home, and the camera was right in front of Sierra's pen. Sierra would climb over, and she looked like a tiny person rock climbing."

Sierra is not allowed to sleep with Sara anymore. "When she was younger, Sierra chewed up more than just my bed covers," Sara says. "At night, she would jump on my bed, and when she was sure that I was asleep, she would start chewing up everything."

Now Sara has new covers and a new rule.

## Insights from the Urban Playground

In San Francisco, siblings sometimes sleep in the same room. San Francisco is only seven square miles and holds more than 884,000 people. Many people share bedrooms.

San Franciscans don't always know their neighbors. Someone can think they are being nice by feeding your lost pet, but they can't ask you whether the food they're giving them is safe.

San Francisco has lots of animals who want a loving home. If you are unlucky enough to lose your pet, you will be sad . . . but when you are ready, many sweet animals would love to live with you.

1. Does anyone in your family wake you up at night?
2. Are you a light sleeper or a heavy sleeper?
3. Have you ever had a pet die?
4. Have you ever blamed yourself for something other people said wasn't your fault?
5. What are the rules in your family?

# Leah, nine years old

Leah, a nine-year-old girl in Mission Terrace, has a thirteen-year-old dog named Marlo, a bichon mix. Marlo was already in the family when Leah, an only child, was born.

"My mom and dad got Marlo in the country, so he doesn't like being in the city much," Leah says. Luckily for Marlo, Leah and her parents take him on road trips to Guerneville, a river town of 4,534 people one-and-a-half hours north of San Francisco where they rent a house some weekends.

San Francisco has 884,363 people, so Guerneville is a little more relaxing for a dog. "Marlo loves Guerneville, but he does not like being in the car," Leah says. "He'll whine the whole way, but he loves it once we get there."

Leah wishes she had a puppy to round out her family. "I really want a Bernese mountain dog because they are super cute and fluffy," she says.

But there is no Bernese mountain dog in Leah's future. "Marlo only has one coat of fur, and Mom is allergic to lots of fur," Leah explains.

Leah wants to be more like Marlo in the way he takes his medicine. "I take this medicine I don't really like, Mucinex, and it takes me ten or fifteen minutes to drink a little bit," she explains.

Not Marlo. "He's a very hurty dog because he's old, so he takes pain medication," Leah says. "He takes it very easily."

Leah has seen the signs of Marlo's aging over the years. "When he gets off the couch, it's hard for him," she says. "And he used to spring down the stairs, but now, he just kind of slips down them."

Marlo's assigned food is dry kibble, Leah says, but the family gives him a lot of treats. "With treats, he listens to you more. If you put a treat in front of him and say, 'Wait,' he will not take the treat, and then you'd say, 'Take it,' and he will take the treat willingly," she says.

Marlo can do other tricks too. "He can fist-bump my dad," Leah says. "My dad will say, 'fist-bump,' and Marlo will put his claw up to my dad's fist." Leah says Marlo mostly follows her dad around the house, "but if somebody's giving him pats on his back, he'll just stay there, needing attention."

One of Leah's favorite things to do in San Francisco is to swim at the newly renovated pool at Balboa Park. Marlo does not swim, Leah says, "but he loves to run and fetch at the beach."

## Insights from the Urban Playground

San Francisco is a nice place for a dog. Fetching at the beach is just one thing dogs can do in the city. They can also go to parks, take urban hikes, and walk through forests . . . all inside San Francisco's seven square miles!

When dogs are older, staying inside and fist-bumping their families might interest them more. Or maybe a little road trip to Guerneville. For an old dog, it can be fun to welcome a new puppy to the family, even if you have to share the family's love.

It's good to have so many options!

---

1. If you were a San Francisco dog, what would be your favorite ways to spend your time?
2. If you could have a puppy, what kind of puppy would you get?
3. What could a dog teach you to do better?
4. What do you think old dogs like to do?
5. If you could teach a dog a fun trick, what would it be?

# WHAT IS YOUR SCHOOL LIKE?

# Seneca, nine years old

Nine-year-old Seneca lives in Duboce Triangle with her mom, dad, and younger sister. She's in third grade.

Seneca's favorite classes are art, PE, and reading. At school, she and her friends create and act out new episodes of the TV show *Dragons: Race to the Edge*.

Seneca wears a school uniform: burgundy pants and a white shirt, or a jumper with patches of burgundy and white, which looks dark pink. Seneca likes her uniform. Her mom and dad take turns driving her to school.

For lunch, the school has a sandwich bar and another bar featuring hot items like potatoes, chili, and toppings. A third area has the main lunch: rice, green beans, and chicken, for example. The school also serves hot bar items like pancakes for breakfast.

Seneca's school has a pen pal program, through which Seneca and her classmates write to fellow third-graders in New York City.

Through the school's language program, Seneca learns one language in the first half of every year, then another in the second half. This year, it's French and Spanish. They change the language sets every two years, except Mandarin, which Seneca's class learned in kindergarten, then they kept learning Mandarin as they also learned Spanish in first grade and French in second.

Seneca's class learns many songs in music class. They just learned "San Francisco (Open Your Golden Gate)." They sang it for their medals assembly, where the school awards medals to students who have done well in certain subjects. "Eight kids get a medal at once," Seneca says. "This time it was math; I didn't get it. Everyone gets a medal for something; it's just a question of what you get it for."

Seneca loves to learn. "You are always finding out a new thing," she says, "and it's kind of fun to brag to your parents that you know it." For example, narwhals—medium-sized toothed whales with large "tusks" from protruding canine teeth—"are unicorns of the sea," Seneca says. "They hide in plain sight. They are a regular thing in our society, but they're unicorns."

Seneca wants to become an author. "I think writing is a really important part of life. If there were no writing, we wouldn't have any recording of history," she says. "The future wouldn't learn anything because they would not have any idea what we've learned."

Her dream is to answer her literary questions through her writing. For example, "In *Harry Potter*, why does Hermione Granger know so much if both her parents are humans? Because in *Harry Potter* world, humans are not supposed to know about the wizarding world."

## Insights from the Urban Playground

Lots of San Francisco kids wear school uniforms, but I don't know how many have pen pals in New York! It's great to have a hot bar at school, and how about those language classes? San Francisco is an interesting city, with many learning opportunities.

And can you believe the city has its own song? The line about opening the city's golden gate is about the Golden Gate Bridge, a beautiful bridge that lets people into San Francisco from the north. Many people have recorded the history of the bridge, and San Francisco is lucky that it still stands today.

# DISCUSSION QUESTIONS

1. If you had a pen pal in another city, what would you write to them about?
2. If you could learn any language in school, what would it be? Why?
3. If your school gave everyone a medal, what would you want to get yours for?
4. What do you like best about your school?
5. If you could answer questions through your writing, what would you answer?

# Brad, nine years old

Nine-year-old Inner Richmond resident Brad is good at math. "Well, I feel like I'm talented in it, so I don't have to pay attention," he says. "Then, when the teacher is like, 'Oh, he's not paying attention' and calls on me, and then I get it right, I feel like, 'In your face, teacher. I don't have to watch and listen.'"

Brad admits that he's a kid with attitude. For example, "If the teacher says, 'Clear your desk,' I'm like, 'My desk is clear, for your information.' But I'm not violent," he says.

Asked whether some kids in his school are violent, Brad answers, "Well, if I counted, there's about ten, but some of those kids are only violent in situations, like some kid got roasted with a yo mama joke, and then he slapped the kid and pushed him down. So that's violent, but that was kind of like a situation."

He adds, "My mom doesn't approve of yo mama jokes. They got banned at school for a long time in third grade. Well, now we're in fourth grade. So what the third-grade teachers say, we don't have to listen."

Does he tell these jokes now? "Well, they're kind of out-dated," he explains. "But when you want to make someone upset, then just use a yo mama joke."

Brad's teacher assigns daily homework. "Normally I'm already a page ahead," he says. "On Monday, I just do four pages. So on the other nights, my homework takes usually less than a minute."

Asked about his favorite things to do in San Francisco, Brad answers, "I enjoy chess tournaments. I play wherever they're hosted." At home, he plays his dad, who usually wins, though Brad has beaten him before. "I like that chess is tricking the opponent, and I think that's strategy, not just luck."

Brad also works as a cashier almost every weekend at the Sunday farmers market near his house. "My mom asked a farmer if I could work for him, and he said yes," he says. "Instead of getting wages, I get fruits."

Is there anything Brad doesn't like about San Francisco? "Well, it's super expensive," he says. "Whenever I want to buy something from my allowance, I have to use up most of my allowance. But I like Amazon because it makes everything cheap."

Asked whether he is allowed to buy from Amazon on his own, Brad answers, "No. Once I tell my dad I want something, he does a day's worth of research. Then, once he's done researching, we just buy what's according to his research."

## Insights from the Urban Playground

San Francisco is expensive, it is true. A kid could easily burn through their allowance in the city, but for workarounds like Amazon and parental research. But with all the technology available in this innovative place, someone who works hard and excels in math can easily thrive.

This is especially true for those who work—like Brad, the weekend farmers market cashier. San Francisco farmers market fruit is expensive, so fruit payment is impressive for a nine-year-old San Franciscan!

Violence arises in many schools . . . not just in San Francisco, but everywhere. It's good to know kids like Brad are paying attention.

---

## DISCUSSION QUESTIONS

1. Are there violent kids in your school, and if so, who are they?
2. Are there any jokes that kids at your school tell that the teachers don't like?
3. Do you ever get ahead of your homework, and if so, how do you do it?
4. What would be fun about chess tournaments, or if you participate in them, what is fun about them?
5. What would you like about working at a weekend farmers market?

# Clinton, five years old

Five-year-old Clinton is in kindergarten at a French school in San Francisco.

"Bonjour!" he says. Switching to English, he says his favorite thing to do at school is to play with his best friend. Clinton's school has two playgrounds, one in the back of the school and the other in front. Clinton likes the back one better because "the more bigger one is the back one."

Clinton likes his teachers. "They are two girls, zero boys. There are actually three girls because my English teacher is a girl," he says. Clinton has two French teachers, who surprise him with what they are going to teach him every day. "They don't really tell me; it's a secret," he says.

He also likes the director of the school. "He doesn't even speak English to me; he does speak a lot of French to me," Clinton says. Teachers never send Clinton to the director's office because he is so well-behaved.

Clinton does not wear a uniform to school; he can wear whatever he wants. "Well, Mama picks my clothes out," he clarifies. "Some people wear boots when it's raining, like I do.

Some people even wear rain jackets when it's raining, like I do. When it's not raining, we just wear our normal shoes. The only uniform I wear is a soccer one," he says.

Clinton plays on the school soccer team, and his jersey number is 10. "It's higher than me," he says.

Clinton says everyone in his class is nice. "I never tell on anyone, but sometimes one of the kids tells on me to the teacher," Clinton adds. "It's not nice, for sure," he says.

Clinton walks to school with his nanny and his sister. At school, he eats the snack and lunch he brings from home—"every kind of snack I really like," he says. His favorite foods to bring are pizza bites, raspberries, blackberries, strawberries, Zebra Cakes, and granola bars.

Clinton does not take naps at school. "I stay awake the whole time," he says. He and his classmates sing songs in French! He does not get any homework.

Clinton says he doesn't want to go to school on the first day. "When it's the second day, I still don't," he adds. "When it's the third day, I think I do, but I don't know. I don't remember. I like it more on the fourth, fifth and sixth and seventh and eighth and ninth," he says.

Clinton says he would like being a teacher, but not of lower grades. "Because then I'd have to teach my sister."

## Insights from the Urban Playground

San Francisco is exciting because you can take classes in many different languages. There are Chinese schools, Spanish immersion schools, German schools, and so many others!

If you went to one of those schools, your teachers would speak to you in the language of another country until that language became natural for you to speak yourself! You might even sing songs in the other language.

In the city, you will meet and learn from people from other cultures. You can bring your own food, like pizza bites, and you can see what people from other countries bring from home too.

---

DISCUSSION QUESTIONS

1. Do you wear a school uniform, pick out your own school clothes, or have a parent pick them out for you?
2. Who takes you to school?
3. What are your favorite snacks to bring to school?
4. Do you take naps at school?
5. Is the first day of school hard for you?

# Olivia, five years old

Five-year-old Olivia gets to school by car. "The drive is two miles or less. Maybe one mile, maybe two miles, maybe three miles," she says. Olivia, an only child, lives in Westwood Highlands when she's with her mom and downtown when she's with her dad.

"Basically, we have hot lunch at school, which I don't like hot things," she adds. "Well, I do like hot things, but not hot lunch because I don't want to be surprised."

Other surprises at Olivia's school include that she no longer takes naps during her school day. "I'm glad I'm not taking naps now because my old school was for little kids," she says. "This school is more serious."

Olivia has an eighth-grade buddy. Olivia shares her buddy with another person in her class, and they meet together with their buddy once a week. Their buddy helps Olivia do arts and crafts and write her name.

Her "regular school class" is Olivia's favorite. There, she creates artwork. Olivia is also learning Spanish. "I just started learning a couple days ago," she says. "Well, a couple weeks ago, or months."

Olivia likes her teacher. "The first thing I like about her is because she starts with *O*, like me," she says, referring to the first letter of her teacher's last name. "And I also like about her that she's really nice to us, and she lets us do really cool things."

Olivia adds, "But there's a twist to the school: we have this thing called the clipboard, which makes you on the clipboard if you get in trouble, and then you're in time-out for twelve or five minutes. Well, for more than that, maybe like ten minutes. And I have never been on the clipboard before, not even one single day."

It's not all about work, though. Olivia's favorite game at school is "American Girl Doll," by which she means playing with her friends, her American Girl doll, and her friends' American Girl dolls. And in her "regular school class," she and her classmates play with magnets, Duplos, and many other toys.

"Also, we have a cat that goes on the road at our school," she says. "Some call him Toby and some call him Rosie. I let the school call him whatever they want. The school hasn't raised the money to buy him a collar yet. Sometimes we get to pet him. Some people are allergic, but I'm not because I have a cat at home."

"My dream is to be a YouTuber," she says. "I have my own YouTube channel."

## Insights from the Urban Playground

In a city of 884,363 people, you'll meet a few whose first or last names begin with *O*. Olivia is lucky to have landed with a teacher who shares her letter!

San Francisco is a good place for a school community to care for an outdoor cat; the weather is nice for a cat who wants to walk around outside. So Rosie or Toby probably has a very happy life.

San Francisco is an international city, interested in places outside the United States and languages other than English . . . so many San Francisco kids learn Spanish in school!

---

1. Do you like to be surprised with a school lunch, or would you rather bring your lunch to school and know what's in it?
2. What do you think you would like about having an older buddy at your school, or if you have one, how do you like the buddy system?
3. What do you think of the system your school uses to handle kids who get in trouble?
4. Do you think the cat at Olivia's school should be named Toby, Rosie, or another name that the school decides?
5. If you had your own YouTube channel, what would you put on it?

# Artin, seven years old

Seven-year-old Artin has a favorite class in school: "Games. We play Ghost in the Graveyard sometimes," he says. "There is three ghosts, and there is these kids that go out, and the ghosts tag them."

Recess is another part of school that Artin loves. "We build these big houses out of crates and boards," he says.

Artin also likes Mandarin and Spanish, two classes he is taking at school. He has a slight preference for Spanish. "We do really fun stuff in Spanish," he explains, "like we play this game where you count to something in Spanish, and whoever moves when you're done counting has to sit down at their desk."

One of Artin's classes is singing. He is learning the song "Bingo"—"*B-I-N-G-O*," he sings.

It is not all about games and songs at Artin's school, which is in Pacific Heights, within walking distance of his dad's house. Artin and his older sister stay together at their dad's house two days a week, then their mom's house in Forest Knolls for another two days, and so on.

The non-games part of his school day includes Mandarin class. "In Mandarin class, we just learn," he says. "And sometimes they make us say words that are a little hard."

According to Artin, school can be an unhappy place for other reasons. "Sometimes people have to sit out of the games," he says. "Mostly, I have to sit out, because I do a little naughty stuff, like talk over the teacher."

Also, though most of the kids in his school are nice to each other, Artin reports that "sometimes they get a little rude. There's a boy that's kind of really mean to all these girls." Artin says these girls like school, but they don't like the way this boy talks to them. "Everybody tells the teacher so he will stop," Artin says.

Artin used to take naps at school. "I liked the naps," he says. "I'm always tired."

Artin plays goalie on his school soccer team, and his preferred sport is tennis, which he plays at Alta Plaza Park.

His sister plays piano and violin, and she sings in a chorus. Artin wants to do the same, "but I'm a little nervous about it, because it's a little hard to do," he says of these musical pursuits.

Artin likes living in San Francisco, "although there are places that are better than San Francisco," he says. "Like Yosemite. There's all this stuff I never saw in San Francisco. The ducks look different in Yosemite; their necks are a little longer."

## Insights from the Urban Playground

Teachers who use games for their lessons obviously make Artin happy, and that's probably true for all kids. San Francisco is filled with creative teachers with good ideas. A game that includes counting in Spanish to teach the lessons? Brilliant! Or should it be "*brillante*"?

San Francisco ducks must have short necks! But you can still see them if you go to the water in San Francisco. They're in ponds around the city and on the beach.

Kids who say mean things are everywhere, including at Artin's school. It is unfortunate, but thankfully, Artin's schoolmates are speaking up about it.

## DISCUSSION QUESTIONS

1. Does Ghost in the Graveyard sound like a fun game to you, or if you've played it, do you think it is fun? Why or why not?
2. What would you do if you heard someone at your school saying mean things to someone else?
3. Do you miss taking naps at school, or if you take school naps now, do you like it? Why or why not?
4. What musical instruments would you be nervous to learn, and why?
5. Where do you think ducks with the longest necks live?

# WHAT SPORTS
# DO YOU PLAY?

# Amalia, nine years old

Nine-year-old Amalia lives in Noe Valley with her little brother and two dads, Daddy and Papa. Amalia plays soccer, tennis, and volleyball, and she swims and surfs.

Amalia plays soccer with the Vikings, a San Francisco club team. "I like soccer because I get to use my feet, and I like my feet better than my hands," she says. She'll play until she is nineteen. "At nineteen, I'm not too young and not too old," she explains. Amalia watches professional women's soccer on TV and looks up to US forward Kelley O'Hara.

For the past month, Papa has given Amalia weekly tennis lessons. Amalia watches professional tennis on TV and admires Serena Williams and fifteen-year-old Cori "Coco" Gauff.

Amalia takes weekly volleyball lessons and will play for nine more years, same as with soccer. For fun, Amalia swims breaststroke at Mission Pool.

Five times a year, Amalia surfs at two San Diego surf camps. "Surfing is harder than it looks," she says. "It's hard to stay on the board and catch the right waves."

In San Diego, Amalia sees her aunt, two uncles, two cousins, and two family dogs. Her family might move there.

"I would miss my house, which is homey because we have a lot of pictures of our family and France in frames," she says.

"I love Paris," she adds. "We never went, but Daddy and Papa downloaded a French language app, and we're working on it together." She can count to ten in French—"*un, deux, trois, quatre, cinq, six, sept, huit, neuf, dix,*"—and can sing the French song "Alouette."

Amalia would miss her friends if she moved. "We have friends that are pretty much like family," she says. But she'd gain a bigger house, flute lessons, and a dog—she's hoping for a yellow lab. "I also like the shopping malls in San Diego," she says. "Malls give you a bunch of choices."

She got the flute idea because her aunt plays. Amalia plays the ukulele and has mastered Taylor Swift's "Shake It Off," a song from the movie *Trolls*, and Smash Mouth's "All Star."

Amalia doesn't play her ukulele for other people. "I don't like attention," she says. What about having spectators at her sports games? "I'm fine with it. In sports, they're paying attention to everyone, not just me," she explains.

Amalia's favorite San Francisco places are Katz Bagels and Mozzeria, a pizzeria whose owners and servers are deaf. "I learned sign language when I was a baby," Amalia says. "I've forgotten it. I only know 'Thank you,' 'milk,' and 'Good morning.'"

## Insights from the Urban Playground

Soccer! Tennis! Volleyball! Swimming! Surfing! It's all available in San Francisco, though San Diego's waves are bigger, so it's easy to see why Amalia would take her surfing lessons there.

San Francisco is the kind of place where you'd find a pizzeria with deaf owners and servers. San Francisco is a big enough city to have a large deaf community, and many San Franciscans like to see and support businesses that value people who face such challenges.

And sports. San Francisco has so many ways to participate in sports . . . and Amalia has obviously taken advantage of those!

1. What do you think would be the best and most challenging parts of being a fifteen-year-old professional athlete?
2. What do you think would be the most fun part of surfing?
3. Would you rather learn sign language, French, or another language, and why did you choose whichever language you did?
4. If you played the ukulele, what would be your favorite song to play, and why?
5. Do you like having attention when you are playing sports or a musical instrument? Why or why not?

# Luca, nine years old

"I eat a lot of protein before my soccer games," says nine-year-old Seacliff resident Luca DeSogos. "I eat eggs with bread and avocado. I drink mostly milk so my bones will be strong."

Luca started taking gymnastics when he was barely walking. He stopped at five years old, when his soccer career took off after he'd been playing for a year.

These days, he plays midfielder and forward for the Vikings, a San Francisco soccer club. He likes having teammates and "being very good enough to score four to five goals in a game."

Among the professional soccer players Luca most admires is Cristiano Ronaldo, who plays for pro soccer club Juventus, and for the Portuguese national team. "Cristiano Ronaldo is cool, and he makes a lot of strong goals," Luca says.

Luca also looks up to Lionel Messi, an Argentine forward and captain of both the Spanish club team Barcelona and the Argentinian national team. "Lionel is the only person in the whole entire world who can dribble without using his feet . . . without touching the ball at all," Luca explains.

Finally, Luca likes Paulo Dybala, an Argentine forward for pro soccer club Juventus and the Argentinian national team. "Paulo scores a lot of goals and makes it look really interesting," Luca says.

Born in San Francisco, Luca is Italian by background. His dad is from Cuglieri in Sardinia, where Luca has visited several times. Luca wants to play professional soccer for Italy someday.

Luca is a red belt, almost brown, in kung fu. He has won the bronze medal for third place. Luca plays basketball and baseball, but not on teams. His favorite basketball players are Steph Curry and Michael Jordan. "Michael Jordan is famous for his slam dunks, and he has shoes," Luca says, referring to Jordan's sneaker line.

Hockey is Luca's second favorite sport, next to soccer. Luca doesn't play hockey, but he went to a college game between a Minnesota team and a New York one and loved it. "I like watching the goalies because it's intense by the goal," he adds.

Luca is not involved in *every* sport. "I have thirty sports that I know," he says. "I want to do running—really, sprinting. It takes fifteen minutes until I get tired out." He wants to improve on that, he says.

"To go pro, the most important thing for me to do is to practice more," Luca says. "Right now, I only practice one to two hours a day."


## Insights from the Urban Playground

San Francisco is a good sports town. Like Luca, many San Franciscans like Warriors point guard Steph Curry, the San Francisco Bay Area pro basketball team. And San Francisco has 220 parks for playing soccer in!

San Francisco kids play many different sports . . . not always as many as Luca, but a lot. San Francisco kids stay busy. If you're a kid in the city who wants to be a pro athlete, San Francisco gives you the best shot because there are so many leagues and lots of other kids in sports. But keeping up with Luca might be tough!

---

1. What do you like to eat before you play sports?
2. How old were you when you started your first sport?
3. Does anyone you know make sports look really interesting?
4. Do you think it would be fun to be Italian by background? Why or why not?
5. If you owned a sneaker line, what kind of sneakers would you have in it?

# *Lilah, nine years old*

Nine-year-old Lilah—who lives in the Castro with her mom, dad, and older sister—plays soccer and gymnastics. "We don't really have positions yet," she says of her soccer club, the Vikings, "but usually I play goalie keeper."

Lilah likes playing goalie. "I prefer using my hands than my feet because I feel like I have more control of my hands than my feet," she explains.

Vikings is not competitive, Lilah says. "Vikings is more about equal playing time. It's nice to have everybody play equally." She adds, "My favorite thing about soccer is that you get to work with a team." And at the end of the season, there is a big party with snacks, cupcakes, and cake.

But soccer is also a lot of work. "It gets really tiring sprinting across the field multiple times," Lilah says. "That's another thing I like about being the goalie: you don't have to sprint around everywhere. When I was younger, the fields were much smaller. Now that I'm nine, the fields are huge."

Another bummer about soccer? Your team doesn't always win. "I mean, it's not that bad, I guess," Lilah says about losing games. "Our coach cheers us on and helps us get through it. It's not great to see the other team cheering and jumping up and down."

Lilah enjoys watching professional soccer. "Usually I watch Brazil games because my mom is pretty much from Brazil," she says. And she watches the World Cup.

"During the Women's World Cup," she says of the 2019 world games, "we were in Sonoma. USA won the Women's World Cup, I'm pretty sure. Everybody was bunched up on the couch. When they won, everybody started jumping up and down."

Asked to identify a pro soccer player she admires, Lilah named Alex Morgan. "She's impressive and really fast," Lilah says.

Lilah loves gymnastics even more than soccer. "I look forward to gymnastics every week," she says. "I think I'll be doing it for a while, unless it gets boring or something."

The best part of gymnastics? "Probably trampoline and tumbling," Lilah says. "Handstands, cartwheels. One of the most impressive things I can do in gymnastics is probably, oh, a headstand or a one-handed roundoff."

Lilah has seen professional gymnastics in person. "I did go to the Olympics in Rio once," she says. "That was cool, I guess."

What does Lilah think would be hard about being a professional gymnast? "If you fall during a competition," she says, "it must be really embarrassing and sad for you because you're knowing that you're just letting your team down."

## Insights from the Urban Playground

San Francisco is a wonderful place to play soccer and perform in gymnastics. Between the opportunities to learn from extremely skilled athletes and some groups' dedication to keeping sports noncompetitive, kids in San Francisco can excel while earning their rewards for fun and teamwork.

The city is full of people from other countries, like Lilah's mom. If you get the opportunity to see the Olympics, especially in another country, you should take it! San Francisco is also a good place to see girls advance in sports; so many girls like Lilah are playing and watching professional female athletes compete.

---

## DISCUSSION QUESTIONS

1. If you play soccer, or if you ever did play, do you think it would be more fun to run around or defend your team's goal, and why?
2. Do you think it would be more fun to play sports in a competitive way or as a team of people supporting each other . . . or can it be both?
3. What sport do you love to play, and what is exciting about it?
4. What would be more fun for you in gymnastics: the trampoline or tumbling?
5. If you could see the Olympics in person in any country, where would you want to see the games?

# Priya, nine years old

Nine-year-old Priya, an only child who lives in Outer Richmond with her mom and in Ingleside with her dad and stepmom, loves playing basketball.

Priya has played basketball for two years. She started playing when her school opened up half of its basketball court at recess for girls who wanted to play. That led to her playing for the school's team.

Priya likes dribbling and shooting, and says her team plays well together. "We're usually really good at passing to each other. I get the ball a lot, and I usually dribble across the court. I've only tried to shoot in a game once, but I didn't make it." What makes someone a good teammate? "They're not a ball hog," Priya says.

One weakness on her team is height. "We're a really short team," explains medium-height Priya, "so when we play against someone else, they're really tall."

Priya wouldn't change anything about basketball, but she says, "It's confusing when they switch the courts after halftime," referring to the rule that each team changes directions halfway through the game, shooting into the other basket for the second half.

"Some people on my team will yell out, 'You're shooting on the wrong hoop!' I know I'm not, but I get confused," she says.

Priya's mom, dad, and stepmom attend Priya's games. Her team is the Wolves. The mascot doesn't show up for games, but sometimes Priya sees the wolf walking the hallway at school. "It's kind of random when it comes out," she says.

Asked how she feels when her team wins, Priya answers, "I don't think we've ever won a game." So how does it feel to lose? "I'm fine. I mean, we're used to it," she says. "We're usually right behind them in points, so we don't ever lose too badly."

Priya's school also has soccer, baseball, and kickball, but none of these interest Priya.

"I did soccer, but I was on a boys' team, so I didn't really like it," Priya says, explaining that she and a friend were the only girls on the team. "My friend kind of dragged me into it because she didn't want to be the only girl there. The boys didn't pass to us."

Priya has no interest in playing professional basketball, but she likes watching pro basketball and soccer games on TV, especially the Women's World Cup. Priya says she doesn't root for any team in particular.

At both her mom's and her dad's houses, Priya has a playground within walking distance. Her favorite thing to do on these playgrounds? "Play basketball."

## Insights from the Urban Playground

San Francisco is a fantastic place to play basketball. The weather is nice, and playgrounds with basketball courts are everywhere, so kids in two homes often have a court nearby with either parent.

Many city schools offer lots of sports. So if you like one sport but not certain others, a school in San Francisco would probably have you covered.

With so many people living in San Francisco, you can find a team of people who share the ball. Priya found hers at school, but there are club teams, rec and parks teams, and several other options outside of school.

---

## DiSCUSSiON QUESTiONS

1. If you were on a basketball team full of short and medium-height people, what could your team do to make up for its lack of height?
2. If you saw someone in a wolf costume pass you in the hallway at school, what would you say to them?
3. Do you think it is important to win at sports games, or would you be happy if you were close in points to the other team, even if you lost?

4. Would you rather play basketball, soccer, baseball, or kickball, and why?
5. If you were a boy on a soccer team of mostly boys, would you pass to the girls? Why or why not?

# *Temby, nine years old*

Nine-year-old Temby plays soccer, baseball, basketball, and karate. A Precita Park resident, he plays sports in neighborhoods all over the city: basketball at a community center, baseball on a league team, and club soccer.

"A good teammate is kind," Temby says. "They have good sportsmanship. When you almost score a goal, they say, 'Nice try. Good job.'"

Temby wants to be a professional soccer player, continuing in his current position of striker. The two pro soccer players he most admires are Cristiano Ronaldo—a forward for pro soccer club Juventus and captain of the Portugal national team—and John Stones, who plays for Premier League club Manchester City and England's national team. Temby says the hardest thing for pro soccer players to deal with is losing the World Cup game.

In basketball, Temby admires Klay Thompson "because Curry and KD get all the credit," Temby says of Steph Curry and Kevin Durant, "but they don't know how to shoot threes like . . . well, Curry might. But Thompson practically makes them every time."

Temby enjoys playing the soccer-themed video games FIFA and FIFA Mobile. He also likes to play Legos at friends' houses, since he does not have any Legos of his own. "Mostly, what happens is, I build Lego structures and put them in the different colored bins, and my little sister destroys what I built."

When he grows up, Temby wants to move out of San Francisco. "The city is just so busy," he says. "On the streets in the Mission, Dogpatch, and Sunset, there are a lot of people. I would like to move to the country."

Though he prefers quiet activities, Temby does not share his mom and dad's appreciation for the San Francisco Museum of Modern Art. But he loves Takoba, the sushi restaurant next to the museum.

"It has delicious sushi," he says. "If I move to the country someday, I would still want to have good sushi, hot dogs, and hamburgers." His favorite place to get hot dogs and hamburgers in the city is Hop Oast Brewpub.

Temby's favorite city parks are Garfield Park, Precita Park, and Dolores Park. "Garfield Park and Precita Park both have huge grass fields, so you can play soccer," he explains. Dolores Park isn't good for playing soccer, he says, but he still likes it there.

Temby is interested in hockey since he likes ice-skating, but he does not play because too many other sports take up his time: he has soccer three days a week; baseball once a week, the same day as soccer; and karate once a week.

## Insights from the Urban Playground

San Francisco is busy, like Temby says. If you like things quiet, you can find the peace you're looking for, but San Francisco is not known for its hushed tones.

There's a lot going on! For one thing, the city has many sports leagues and clubs, with kids going all across town to get to practice and games.

There are also many museums and restaurants, like the San Francisco Museum of Modern Art and the nearby sushi restaurant. The parks are fantastic, and the weather is usually good for soccer. There's a lot in San Francisco to make noise about!

1. What do you think makes someone a good teammate?
2. If you were going to be a professional athlete, what sport would you choose?
3. Do you like busy cities or quieter places better, and why?
4. What is your favorite thing to do in the park?
5. If there is any activity that interests you that you're not doing now, what is it?

# WHAT ARE
# YOUR TALENTS?

# Aleksey, nine years old

Nine-year-old Aleksey is a yellow belt in jujitsu. His talents extend beyond martial arts.

"I am good at making things with Legos, and I like to make action movies," he says. "I'm also good at basketball, soccer, and sometimes kickball, if you know that game."

Aleksey lives in the Mission Bay neighborhood near the ballpark, in a big apartment building with his mom and his grandma. He has friends in the building, which also has a gym and a kids' center.

Aleksey gets around by Muni train and Uber. He takes Muni to his school, where he excels in art, computers, PE, and dance.

In first grade, Aleksey performed a solo play in front of his whole school and felt very nervous. The next year, when he danced in a group recital for the same audience, he was not afraid.

Being onstage with others helped Aleksey. Also, the crowd behaved differently the second time. "The first year, people didn't clap because they were looking at their phones," he explains.

Aleksey's classmates occasionally miss out on his talents. "Last year, I was very, very good at climbing," he says. "So I tried to do some very hard monkey bars. I have a lot of friends in my school, but they didn't really compliment me. They said nothing."

Aleksey's favorite San Francisco places are Mission Creek Park, the Mission Bay and West Portal libraries, comic book stores, and the Metreon movie theater. He also likes Italian, American, Mexican, Japanese, and seafood restaurants and the mall, where he frequents the LEGO Store and the "Xbox Store," his name for the Microsoft Store.

Aleksey likes San Francisco's tall buildings. "I'll tell you why," he says. "Because you can actually get more of a big view." He has wanted to go in the Transamerica Pyramid since he was six years old, and he also has his eye on the Salesforce Tower.

Aleksey sometimes crosses the Bay Bridge by car to visit his dad, who lives in Oakland. "A lot of times, I'll talk to him on the phone," he says. "But sometimes he invites me to his house, and we have a good time.

"I would say I like San Francisco, but some people here are very crazy. They say a lot of curse words, and then they throw stuff for no reason," Aleksey says.

"If you are on Mission Street," he adds, "it smells bad, like tobacco. But I know this barbecue place somewhere next to Mission Street. Once you get closer to that place, it smells like fresh barbecue. And there is always the sunny weather."

## Insights from the Urban Playground

San Francisco is a special place: tall buildings, nice weather, taking the bus to school, and lots of interesting smells! Can you imagine living in a big building with your friends down the hall and your grandma in your apartment?

With all the people in San Francisco, it can be hard to notice someone climbing on the monkey bars or performing onstage, even if they're super talented. Sometimes people in the city have to put their phones down and pay attention. When you work hard to show your talents to your schoolmates, it feels great when they burst into applause.

---

DISCUSSION QUESTIONS

1. Do you like martial arts?
2. Would you like taking the bus to school?
3. Do you feel nervous when you perform on a stage?
4. Are you good at climbing on monkey bars?
5. What smells do you notice where you live?

# Anjali, five years old

~eue~

Five-year-old Anjali is good at reading Elephant and Piggie books. "I made up a book called *I Love Pig Party*," she says, "where a bunch of different animals dressed up as pigs throw pigs in the air."

Anjali can make up other stories too. "Once upon a time, in a faraway land, there lived one goat who could tell time and one pig and one girl named Little Red Riding Hood," she says. "The pig would have a microscope."

What does Anjali love about reading? "If you read," she says, "you get to learn about all the things in the book. It's not only the pictures that help you."

Anjali, who lives in the Mission with her mom, dad, and two younger sisters, is also talented at drawing. "I really like drawing the most," she says.

Anjali speaks well in front of her class. At school, she and her classmates present story journals, including a "Monday journal," in which they share what they did over the weekend, with a teacher's help writing down their stories.

"I'm good at cheering friends on. That's what I am mostly good at," Anjali says. "In this class called PE, where you do a lot of throwing and running and losing, I cheer my friends on. It's nice, and it helps them be brave.

"I'm good at doing the math," she adds. "I'm the goodest at math, so I have to do the most work." Her teacher keeps handing out work as she and her fellow students get it done, Anjali explains, so she gets more than others because she moves through math quickly.

"Oh, and yarn, sewing, and Legos," Anjali says. She excels in these areas too.

"I'm not good at ice-skating," she says. "I haven't done it yet. I will do it this Christmas in Tahoe."

Tahoe is a lake community of 21,978 people that gets snow and ice in the winter. That's compared to 884,363 in San Francisco, which does not get snow or ice. Speaking of Tahoe, Anjali says she can also flip on her skis.

Anjali's favorite thing to do in San Francisco is "to go across the Golden Gate Bridge because it's so beautiful," she says. "I like the Golden Gate Bridge because it reminds me of a certain animal: a fox is orange, just like the Golden Gate Bridge." But a fox is not Anjali's favorite animal. A rabbit is.

Anjali whispers that she is talented at making flags and will make a flag for her little sister's next birthday as a surprise gift.


## Insights from the Urban Playground

The Golden Gate Bridge and foxes share the color orange, that's true. But can a bunch of animals dressed as pigs throw pigs in the air? That seems unlikely! But if that can happen anywhere, it would be San Francisco.

San Francisco is a magical place, full of people with vivid imaginations, big dreams, and huge talent, like Anjali. Is there anything she can't do? I don't think so! Well, maybe something she hasn't tried, like ice-skating. But since she lives so close to Tahoe, she will soon have her chance to master that too.

# DiSCUSSiON QUESTiONS

1. If you were an animal and you went to a pig party dressed as a pig, what animal would you be underneath your costume?
2. If you kept a story journal, what types of stories about your life would you put in it?
3. Are you good at cheering your friends on, and are they good at cheering you on?
4. Looking at a picture of the Golden Gate Bridge, what animal does it remind you of?
5. If you made a surprise birthday gift for someone using your talents, what would you make, and for whom would you make it?

# Thomas, six years old

Six-year-old Thomas Otero likes regular school "a little better" than preschool. "The park where I can play is bigger," he says, referring to his school's playground.

Thomas lives with his mom and dad in the Western Addition. He mostly goes to Alta Plaza and Golden Gate Park. "I like to go on trails with my bike," he says.

The family has three cars. One for each person? "Yes. I drive the sports car," Thomas jokes. Does he ever walk anywhere? "Yes, lots."

Asked what his talents are, Thomas replies, "Let's see. There's a long list." First on that register is math, which Thomas likes because "sometimes I can't do it on my fingers, so it's more challenging."

He is also good at reading, and he likes to read "short books with lots of short words in them, I guess." Thomas frequents two libraries: one close to his school and San Francisco's main library, the Civic Center library. Thomas can walk to his school's library from campus, "but it would be a bit far," he says.

When Thomas wants books for purchase, he visits Green Apple Books. What type of books does he prefer? "I like fact books," he says, explaining that he likes learning interesting facts about the world and teaching them to his parents.

Thomas is a talented writer. "I do write stories," he says, adding that his favorite type to write are "real-life stories about my life."

Thomas is an excellent athlete too. "I'm good at soccer. I'm good at swimming. And I'm kind of good at baseball," he says. He likes playing defense on his soccer team. "I get to wait until the ball comes because I can get ready," he explains.

He knows he is a strong swimmer because "one time I raced freestyle against my mom, but she beat me, but I was really close at beating her." He has taken lessons for five years. What pools does Thomas swim in? "That's so hard," he says, pausing to think. "I swim at La Petite Baleen and the Palace Hotel."

Asked what baseball position he likes to play, Thomas answers, "I think I would say the batting part." What about on the field? "I would say defense," he says. "No, I would say actually outfield."

If someone were visiting San Francisco, Thomas would suggest they visit the Salesforce Tower, the highest building in San Francisco at sixty-one floors. Thomas has been up to the top, and he says, "Go up and see the view, especially my dad, because I want to see that. He's scared of heights."

## Insights from the Urban Playground

Salesforce Tower is impressive, cutting through a skyline that is quite low as big cities go. Thomas is brave to visit the top at only six years old!

In San Francisco, you'll find many multitalented kids like Thomas. There's so much to do—lots of lessons to take, teams to join, and parks to play in. Children in San Francisco can really develop their talents in such a stimulating environment.

Green Apple Books is a San Francisco treasure. And the Civic Center library is huge and full of books! There, Thomas can find so many facts to share with his parents.

## DISCUSSION QUESTIONS

1. What do you think is the best thing about math?
2. If you could teach your parent(s) any fact, what would it be, and why?
3. If you like to write stories or want to when you're older, what type of stories do you or would you like to write, and why?
4. Can you beat your parent(s) at swimming?
5. What is the highest floor in a building that you would want to go up to?

# Eloise, eight years old

Eight-year-old Eloise is a talented reader who prefers chapter books and admires people who can read quickly.

"One of my friends used to be on the third *Harry Potter* book when I was in the beginning of the fourth book, but now she's ahead of me in the fourth book," she says. "I'm mind blown."

Eloise is also a talented actor who makes up plays with her cousins when they visit her in San Francisco or she goes to New Jersey, where they live.

"One of the ones we're doing is *Beauty and the Beast*," she says. "We might not have enough people for one scene, since there are only three of us." They have also written an original play—a mystery called *School Mystery*.

Eloise has also been to the theater: she has seen *Annie* in San Francisco and *High School Musical* in New Jersey. She also gets to see all the dress rehearsals for plays at her school, which she is too young to perform in because only fourth- through eighth-graders get to be in the school plays, and Eloise is in third grade. Recent dress rehearsals she has seen were for *Shrek* and *Suessical*, a mix of Dr. Suess stories told in one play.

Eloise wants to be a professional actor when she grows up. To the question of whether she wants to be onstage, in movies, or on TV, Eloise replies, "I want to be all sorts of actors. On TV or something like that, or movies or something. At least an actor, though."

Would she star in funny, sad, scary, or mysterious productions? "Mysteries and funny things," she says. "Maybe some things combined. You should have three things combined together, and that would make a wonderful story."

Eloise says babies can be talented. "It depends what type of baby," she explains. "If they were a day old, I don't think they could really do that many things at all. But most babies start walking at a certain age, so a talented baby could start walking at a very early age."

Eloise lives in the Outer Sunset with her mom, dad, and younger sister. She likes walking around her neighborhood—"going on miniature little adventures," as she says. For dinner, she likes to pick up either sushi, pizza, or rice and dumplings near her house. She loves to visit libraries, bookstores, and the Children's Creativity Museum.

Eloise and her family take ferry tours under the Golden Gate Bridge. "We did that ride during whale season, and a whale came one yard away from the boat," she says.

## Insights from the Urban Playground

San Francisco has a beautiful bridge: the Golden Gate Bridge, whose color is called "international orange." If you live in or visit San Francisco, you can take a ferry tour under the bridge like Eloise and her family have done. If you're lucky, whales might swim near your boat!

With its nice weather and its many shops and restaurants, San Francisco is a very walkable city. It's the perfect place to go on miniature little adventures. The food is spectacular, the people are friendly, and you can even walk to the theatre . . . as long as you have a ticket!

DISCUSSION QUESTIONS

1. What is a talent you wish you had that you don't have yet?
2. Do you think you would like making up your own play? Why or why not?
3. What do you think a talented baby could do?
4. If you could walk right outside your house into a miniature little adventure, what activities would you choose?
5. If you could take a ferry tour, where would you want to go?

# Lex, eight years old

Eight-year-old Lex lives in an enchanted forest . . . Sherwood Forest, that is. Well, he doesn't live *in* the forest, but he lives very close.

Lex, an only child, likes to act, sing, and dance. He wants to be a movie actor when he grows up. At acting camp last summer, he played Demeter in *The Myth of Persephone and Demeter*, a play he performed for his mom and dad, and all the other acting camp parents.

"I get nervous before every performance," Lex says, "but I always feel great afterward because it goes really well."

Lex used to take hip-hop dancing lessons in the Mission, and he wants to improve at hip-hop, the only form of dancing that interests him. He says practicing is the only thing that will help him get better.

Lex is a talented baseball player. Asked what position he plays best, he answers, "Hitting." He and his parents are huge Giants fans. They go to baseball games when the company his mom works for gives them tickets to a suite at Oracle Park, the ballpark where the Giants play.

"I always love it when that happens," Lex says, "because the popcorn and peanuts are free." Lex also likes to eat ice cream sundaes at the ballpark, even when the weather is cold.

Lex named his three-year-old dog Buster after his favorite Giants player, Buster Posey. "I thought of the name at a Giants game," Lex says.

Buster is a terrier mix who has been in Lex's family since Buster was two weeks old. "I taught Buster to sit and stay while I walk away with his dog treat," Lex says. Buster mastered the trick without ever going to a professional dog trainer, Lex adds.

Lex says babies can be talented. At what? "Being cute," he answers. "I see a lot of babies walking around San Francisco."

Lex likes living in San Francisco. "I like that it's a big city," he says. "I like the tall buildings. San Francisco has more concrete, more metal, more glass than Portugal and Hawaii," two places Lex visited last summer. But he thinks San Francisco needs more trees.

Lex loves to go to Cuppa, a juice bar in Glen Park that serves boba tea and musubi. "Musubi is seaweed with rice on the top, rice on bottom, and spam in the middle," he explains. "It's delicious."

## Insights from the Urban Playground

San Francisco has camps and lessons for anything that interests you, like acting and dancing for Lex. It is a great city for advancing your natural talents and developing new ones.

Many talented people in San Francisco serve food from other cultures, like the juice bar Lex likes that serves Japanese food.

The city also has talented baseball players you can name your dog after, like Buster Posey. Giants games are so much fun. Oracle Park has the standard ballpark popcorn and peanuts Lex mentioned, but also those sundaes he likes . . . and even sushi, Chinese food, and cheese plates!

**DiSCUSSiON QUESTiONS**

1. What would you like best about living near a forest?
2. Do you get nervous before performing or speaking in front of big groups, and how do you feel afterward?
3. If you could have any food at a baseball game, what would you want to eat, and why?
4. What do you think would be the hardest thing about training your own dog?
5. What would you do if you saw a baby walking around where you live?

# WHERE DO YOU GO

# ON VACATION?

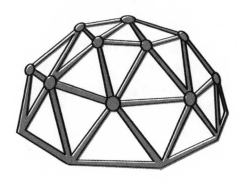

# William, eight years old

William, an eight-year-old boy in West Portal, vacations in Lake Tahoe every year with his mom, dad, twin sister, and older brother.

In Tahoe, William loves being in nature: hiking, riding bikes, and outdoor rock climbing. William says people in Tahoe are nice. "Like when we go on hikes with our cousins there, and we get lost, they give us directions."

William thinks people in Tahoe are happy because they have lots of trees around them, "and because it is hot there in the summer and cold in the winter, the opposite of San Francisco."

William says that when Tahoe people visit San Francisco, they go to the Golden Gate Bridge and Pier 39. They also visit the wax museum or the Ripley's Believe It or Not! museum, two of William's favorite places. William also likes to go to Pier 39 to watch the seals who live in the water there.

"People who visit San Francisco think it has a lot of famous landmarks and that it is a large city," William says, "because they come here from smaller places."

This summer, William's family went to visit his first au pair in Germany, where she lives now. Then they went to Paris, where they saw the Eiffel Tower, the Arc de Triomphe, and the Louvre.

"Paris is a big city, a worldwide city, and it has a lot of famous landmarks," William says. Just like in Tahoe, people in Paris are nice because they helped William's family when they were trying to find their way somewhere. He thinks the people who live there work mostly in restaurants and in construction.

William wants to return to Paris since they were there only two days and did not get to see everything. William wants to visit their soccer stadium.

William's family took a train from Paris to London. "We sat in very comfortable chairs," he says of the ride. London people are nice, William says, because they gave directions, like people in Paris did. Are people in London happy? William answered, "Yeah, because they have a wax museum." When William was there, Big Ben, London's biggest clock, was under construction.

For his next vacation, William and his family will travel to São Paulo, Brazil, to visit his second au pair, who lives there now. William misses his first and second au pairs very much, and he likes his third au pair, who is from Rio de Janeiro and takes care of him now in San Francisco.

William says the only bad thing about vacation is packing. "We waste a lot of our day."

## Insights from the Urban Playground

San Francisco is full of famous landmarks. There are William's favorites—the Golden Gate Bridge and Pier 39—plus

Mission Dolores, Ghirardelli Square, City Hall, the Palace of Fine Arts, the Castro Theatre, the Flatiron Building, Coit Tower, Grace Cathedral, Beach Chalet, the Fairmont Hotel, Spreckels Mansion, Mount Davidson, Washington Square Park . . . oh, and the wax museum!

If you're visiting San Francisco, you can easily get into nature if you know where you're going. People who know their way around the city can be so nice, showing you on maps or phone apps how to get where you're trying to go.

DISCUSSION QUESTIONS

1. When you've been on vacation, did the people who live there seem happy?
2. What do you think people like about the place you live when they visit?
3. What are some famous landmarks you've seen on vacation?
4. If you were choosing someplace to go on vacation, what would you want to do there?
5. Do you like packing for vacation? Why or why not?

# Ella, eight years old

"I was born in the year of the rabbit," says Ella, an eight-year-old Alamo Square resident. This summer, she traveled to Ireland and Italy with her mom, dad, and older sister.

Ella takes Ukranian and Mexican dance lessons in San Francisco. While in Ireland, she performed with her dance company and saw professional Irish dancers live. "It must have taken them twenty years to get good at it," Ella says.

In Ireland, Ella and her family spent their time in Cork and Killarney. "I ate a lot of burgers and french fries," Ella says. "The burgers were mostly good, but some of them had fat in them, which I didn't like. But the fries were good. Also, I learned that in Ireland, 'chips' means 'french fries.'"

Another lesson for Ella? That in Ireland, everyone drives on the left side of the road, not the right as in San Francisco.

In Italy, the family explored Basilicata, Nova Siri, and Rome. In Basilicata, they stayed in a trulli. "Trullis are houses that they made out of brick," she explains. "And when the taxes came from the king, the people took their trullis apart so they didn't have to pay their taxes. And once the taxes were over, they just rebuilt them."

In Nova Siri, Ella saw her cousins and played at a fountain. "The water came from a mountain, and it was cold, and Italy was really hot," Ella adds. "You could drink from the spout, and if you put your thumb on the place where the water came out, the water would go spraying everywhere. I made several water rainbows, and we soaked our dad."

In Rome, the family toured the Colosseum. "We could see where the gladiators fought," she says, "but since it was made out of wood and then sand on top, the wood was all rotted away."

She loved the gelato in Rome, mostly ordering lemon and strawberry. "In San Francisco, I get my gelato from a place called Bi-Rite. It's like a supermarket, but it also sells ice cream. I really like the birthday cake flavor," she says.

Ella's family goes to New Jersey every Christmas to celebrate with her mom's side of the family, who are Italian. Ella says she can understand most of the Italian language, but that her Italian speaking needs work.

She also goes horseback riding at her family's Geyserville vacation home. Ella doesn't own a horse, but she always rides a brown horse named Ice. "Ice is very kind and sweet," Ella says. "But also, when it's sunny, he likes taking naps."

## Insights from the Urban Playground

Bi-Rite is a fabulous place for ice cream . . . it's true! And San Francisco has two locations, so there's even more ice cream to love. Birthday cake flavor, even! How wonderful.

If you want to improve upon your Italian language skills, you can find lots of people to speak it with in San Francisco. There's a community of people who are from Italy or have family members from there.

And the Ukranian and Mexican dance lessons . . . those are just two of many dances you can learn. Maybe, like Ella, your hard work will take you to stages in Europe.

---

**DISCUSSION QUESTIONS**

1. If you could perform any kind of dance anywhere in the world, what type of dance would you choose and where would you do it?
2. What do you think it would be like to see a bunch of people driving on a different side of the road than you're used to seeing?
3. If you could soak anyone with a Roman water fountain, who would you pick?
4. What language would you like to learn, and why?
5. If you could go horseback riding at a country vacation home, what would you want your horse's name to be, and what would your horse's personality be like?

# *Zachary, six years old*

Six-year-old Zachary, born on the Fourth of July, loves fireworks. "I like it when the finale goes," he says, "because the fireworks go 'boom, boom, boom.'"

Zachary, who lives in San Francisco's Miraloma Park neighborhood with his mom and dad, and who has an older stepsister and stepbrother living outside their home, remembers seeing fireworks while on vacation in Peru.

But it could have been somewhere else, he says. Zachary has also vacationed in Hawaii, England, Mexico, and Australia.

In Hawaii, "I had a lot of ice cream every day," Zachary says. At an ice cream shop near his hotel, he ordered his favorite flavor, candy. "And I got to see some goats and keep a goat," he adds. "But then I let it free."

He also snorkeled. "I got in the water and I swimmed very deep," he says. "Probably near the deepest part of the ocean."

When he was five, Zachary saw llamas on a farm in England. He sat on a white-and-brown llama but did not ride it. "It was the dad," Zachary says. Was he gentle? "Yeah, he doesn't bite, and he doesn't kick." He also saw guinea pigs and bears.

Of the weather in England, Zachary says, "It was always sunny since it was all the way on the top of the earth."

In Mexico, people were speaking Spanish, and Zachary had fun learning the language. "It came a little easy," he says, "but then it came a little harder, and then when I just got the hang of it, it was easier."

Australia was fun because Zachary visited his grandparents. His mom was born and raised in Australia, and her parents still live there. While visiting, Zachary saw kangaroos. "They were brown and blue," he says. "I saw one with a little baby in a pouch. I petted it. The mom was not so mad."

For Zachary, the most fun activity in Australia was going on a boat with his grandparents. "I saw some fishes, and I took some pictures, and I petted the beautiful ones, like the unicorn fish," he says. He also pet a sea turtle's shell.

Back in San Francisco, one of Zachary's favorite pastimes is "to look at the artwork I make," he says. "I can make a rhino, and I can draw a horse and a moose. Also, I make two artworks that look the same, one that a person gets, and the other one's for me." He says he sells his pieces for $25 each, then gives them to people living on San Francisco's streets.

### Insights from the Urban Playground

There are all sorts of interesting animals all over the world and San Francisco artists like Zachary who feature animals. Giving his art away to people who can't afford it is a lovely act of kindness. San Francisco is full of people like Zachary who are kind to poor people in the city.

San Francisco has Spanish speakers, but not everywhere. Vacationing in a place where you can get the hang of a new language would be great fun. You can learn to snorkel in San Francisco, but I don't know about going near the deepest part of the ocean!

---

1. If you could vacation in Peru, Hawaii, England, Mexico, or Australia, where would you want to go first, and why?
2. What language would you want to learn on vacation?
3. Would you want to pet a kangaroo with a baby in her pouch?
4. What is the most beautiful fish you can imagine, and what does it look like?
5. If you could make something, sell it, and give it away to someone living on the street, what would you create?

# Silas, nine years old

Every two years, nine-year-old Silas spends spring break at the beach and a pool in Naples, Florida, where his paternal grandma lives six months out of the year.

Silas lives in Bernal Heights with his mom, dad, and younger sister, and will soon be in fourth grade.

Silas swims monthly in San Francisco, often at his friends' birthday parties. He has been swimming at the UCSF campus near the new Warriors stadium, at the Garfield Pool, and at the Balboa Pool.

Naples is hotter than San Francisco, Silas says. He prefers Naples because "it's easier to get your parents to do stuff," like going to air-conditioned movie theaters in ninety-five-degree weather.

The other half of the year, Silas's grandma lives in a Washington, DC, suburb in Virginia, where the family goes every Thanksgiving. Unlike San Francisco, DC is cold, Silas says; he has been there in forty-five-degree weather. "DC has a lot more old revolutionary things, like Mount Vernon," Silas says.

Silas's family parasailed in Sayulita, Mexico, one Christmas. They have also taken a ferry from Seattle to Whidbey

Island, flown to San Diego for a family reunion on his mom's side, and skied in Vail, Colorado.

They visit Silas's maternal grandma and grandpa, Mimi and Pa, in the woods of Asheville, North Carolina, and at Mimi and Pa's second home in Kiawah Island, South Carolina.

When Silas was six, "we went all out and went to Barcelona for three weeks and Amsterdam for three weeks," Silas says.

In Barcelona, they stayed within two blocks of an ice cream shop and a park. In Amsterdam, they toured the Anne Frank House. "I thought, *Oh my god, what if there's a war?*" he says.

This summer, Silas's family will stay in a mansion in Ireland for a family reunion on his dad's side and will rent an old house in London.

On living in San Francisco, Silas says, "It is really nice. But some places, there are a lot of sketchy-looking people. My dad is trying to get me to walk to Precita Park Café from our house by myself and buy a cookie. But it doesn't feel safe to do that. I am working on it."

Precita Park is Silas's favorite park; his sister likes South Park. Their family frequents Bernal Library and the Cortland Playground.

Silas says people who visit San Francisco should hike Mount Davidson. They should also go to the Mission for ice cream at Bi-Rite and a movie and cookie at the Alamo Drafthouse, he says. Silas thinks visitors will love San Francisco's sculptures and food.

## Insights from the Urban Playground

San Francisco has great weather: not Naples hot, not DC cold. There are lots of great pools around the city that you can use since people don't usually have pools at home like many in Naples do. Like Silas says, there are nice parks for playing, great city hikes, and wonderful food. But city life doesn't always feel safe.

Vacations can provide good lessons, like DC's rich American Revolution history. And Amsterdam's Anne Frank House teaches visitors about World War II. San Francisco has historical sites of its own, but many attractions in those places are modern.

---

# DISCUSSION QUESTIONS

1. Where do you think it would be fun to swim?
2. Would you rather visit a hot or cold weather place, and why?
3. What would be the best thing about a ferry ride?
4. What would you most like to learn about through a vacation?
5. What would be the best place to go for a family reunion?

# Ella Grace, seven years old

Seven-year-old Ella Grace, who lives in the Mission with her mom and dad, vacations in Italy, New York, New Jersey, San Diego, and Arizona.

Asked where in Italy she has traveled, Ella Grace answers, "Basically all the parts." Her mom's parents and her cousins live there.

Ella Grace loves to eat pasta and soup in Italy, and her favorite two items from the trip were a bracelet and a key chain with a bear on it. For the past five years, Ella Grace has been taking Italian classes to keep her language skills strong.

In Europe, Ella Grace's family stays in hotels. Her favorite thing about hotel stays is "that there's breakfasts, and it's free." She also likes eating yogurt or pie for breakfast, something she never does at home.

In Arizona, Ella Grace has stayed at her friend's house. "And I went to his friend's birthday party. I drove the fire truck. And I believe that's it," she says. "Phoenix was really, really, really, really, really, really, really, really, really, really hot."

In New Jersey, Ella Grace went to the beach. "I'm there every day," she says. "I would go into the ocean, sunbathe, play, make sand castles, and that's it."

Ella Grace says she stayed with her friend in New Jersey and slept in a bunk bed. The house was within walking distance of the beach. Ella Grace wishes she could walk to the beach from her San Francisco home.

Ella Grace has also been to New York five times. "It's a pretty place," she says. "It's the same as San Francisco, but New York has more ocean. Ocean, ocean, ocean, ocean, ocean, ocean, ocean, ocean."

In San Diego, Ella Grace visited her aunt, "and my mom's brother's kids, and that's it," she adds. "New Jersey has the cleanest beaches, then San Diego, then San Francisco."

Back home in San Francisco, Ella Grace likes going to Mission Park. "I go down the slide and do the obstacle course," she says, "and I go through the sprinklers." She thinks adults would like Mission Park because "there's an ice cream man," and adults can play tennis or swim in the park.

For her next vacation, Ella Grace wants to go to Germany. "My friend goes there every summer, and I think she says she likes Germany a lot," Ella Grace says. "So I think I want to go there."

When she grows up, Ella Grace wants to live in San Rafael, a suburb north of San Francisco. "It's way cleaner," she says, "and there's no sidewalks, so it means less busier."

## Insights from the Urban Playground

San Francisco beaches could always be cleaner, but they are pretty nice. Lots of people clean them up on the weekends, not because it is their job, but because they love San Francisco and the environment, and they want to keep the city clean and the earth shipshape. But New Jersey and San Diego people must be doing it better!

Ice cream trucks in the park are the best. And tennis and swimming! While San Francisco parks are great, wouldn't it be wonderful to visit Italy and know how to speak with the locals, and eat free hotel breakfasts?

**DiSCUSSiON QUESTiONS**

1. If you went to Italy, what would be your favorite thing to bring back?
2. Would you want to visit someplace really, really, really hot like Arizona? Or if you live in a hot place, would you want to visit someplace really, really, really cold? Why or why not?
3. Do you think the place where you live is clean, and how could it get cleaner?
4. If you saw someone selling ice cream from a truck in the park, what kind would you get?
5. Where do you want to take your next vacation, and why?

# WHEN YOU GROW UP, WHAT DO YOU WANT YOUR JOB TO BE?

# Jazmin, eight years old

Eight-year-old Jazmin wants to be a baker when she grows up. Jazmin, who lives in the Mission with her mom, dad, older brother, and older sister, wants to work hard like her parents do: Her mom cleans houses and takes care of two kids, and her dad cooks Mexican food in a restaurant.

Jazmin will specialize in ice cream cakes and milk chocolate cakes. "I don't like dark chocolate cakes," she explains. She will also make animal cakes, featuring puppies, bears, lions, and tigers. Her favorite ice cream cake to bake would feature Oreo chocolate, then Oreo vanilla. "It would be fun to do all those layers," she says.

Jazmin wants to be her own boss. "When people are my boss, they could scream at me," she says. She does not want employees, except maybe her mom, with whom she bakes now. "My mom knows how to make cakes but usually uses the one that comes in a box. I would teach her to make cakes," Jazmin says. "This doesn't count as a cake, but I make banana bread with my mom," she says.

Before aspiring to be a baker, Jazmin wanted to be a professional gymnast or a soccer player. She takes gymnastics outside of school and plays goalie and defender on her school soccer field.

Jazmin switched career goals when she started watching baking videos on her mom's phone. "I don't have to run and move a lot to be a baker," she says. "I just have to find materials I want to use to make my cakes and cookies." Plus, Jazmin doesn't like that climbing on the monkey bars callouses her hands.

Jazmin wants to open her bakery in Paris, France, where she will live full-time, traveling four weeks a year to Hawaii and Mexico for two weeks each. "I'm done with San Francisco," she says. "Most of the schools and parks are pretty, but it ruins it when people throw their garbage on the floor." She likes the Presidio's spinning play structure and, at Crissy Field, the basketball and tennis courts and the grass, where she does gymnastics.

Jazmin was born in San Francisco, "but I'm a little bit Mexican because of my mom and dad," she says. Her parents were born in Toluca, Mexico.

This summer, she will visit Mexico with her sister, brother, and cousin. "We're going one day after my mom's birthday," she says. "I'm nervous to see if I cry because I will be away from my parents for so long. They can't go because they don't have passports to come back."

## Insights from the Urban Playground

San Francisco has many grassy spaces for gymnastics. Sometimes there is garbage on the floor, which is too bad because the parks are beautiful. Some people pick up garbage, even though it is not their job, because they want to help San Francisco look pretty.

Lots of San Francisco kids have parents born in other countries. Some of those kids, like Jazmin, can't go with their parents to see where they grew up since their parents couldn't return to the United States if they left. Jazmin is lucky that her older siblings and cousin can take her to Mexico.

---

# DISCUSSION QUESTIONS

1. What would be fun about owning a bakery?
2. Would it be more fun to play professional sports or to have a job where you didn't have to run as much?
3. Why do you think people leave garbage on the ground?
4. Do you like spinning play structures?
5. What would it be like for you to travel without your parents?

# Travis, nine years old

Nine-year-old Bernal Heights resident Travis has given his future career some thought. "I was thinking about maybe being a cop," he says.

Travis, who is hearing impaired and lives with his mom, dad, and deaf older brother, likes adventure. "I think you get a good sum of money from being a cop," he says, "and you still get a lot of action while you're getting money too."

What does Travis think a typical day for a cop would be? "Well, I have about two theories for that," he says. "The first one is, a cop could be one of the suspects in a trial for the criminal if they get caught. The other thing they do is they work at a desk job, figuring out stuff that's happened."

He adds, "Honestly, sometimes it could be a little boring, 'cause if you go into a cop station in a nice little neighborhood with home security, that's unlikely to get burglars, so you could just be sitting at your desk, sipping a coffee all day, and you can get a donut. Then you get stuck with a desk job."

What does Travis think cops are like in general? "They'd probably have to go through a lot of training to be a cop, so they'd probably be super strong and tough. So they might grunt a lot."

As for the type of cop he would be, Travis says, "I'd probably be really tough, too, but I don't really grunt. I would be cheerful-slash-tough." If people were giving out awards for their cop service, Travis says his award would be for "maybe running after a criminal. I run really fast."

Travis also suspects his lunch routine would differ from that of most cops. "In most movies, I see cops get Chinese food for some reason," he says. "I like Chinese food, too, but it's not healthy. I'd probably at least eat five peeled carrots a day for lunch, to get better eyesight. And then I'd also have maybe a ham and cheese sandwich with mayonnaise."

Travis says his mom creates software, "and my dad's explained to me what he's done, but I've never really known what he's done." Both have desk jobs, he explains, and "they would probably get a lot more money than me, but they wouldn't get any action or adventure."

Does anything scare Travis about being a cop? "Oh, yes," he answers. "If they outnumber you, you have a bunch of criminals surrounding you, and if you don't know karate or kung fu, you're going to get captured."

## Insights from the Urban Playground

San Francisco has a lot of action for a cop. There would not be much time to eat Chinese food and donuts, or to sip coffee all day. The city is just too busy for that! And it is a good place to learn karate or kung fu to supplement your official police training; there are many places in the city to take lessons.

In San Francisco, there's not too much to grunt about for a cop. The city has many home security systems, but there are also lots of criminal courtrooms where cops can serve as trial witnesses.

---

**DiSCUSSiON QUESTiONS**

1. What do you think would be fun about being a police officer?
2. When you grow up, do you want a job where it's slow enough for you to eat donuts and sip coffee, or would you rather have lots of action, and why?
3. When you grow up and have a job, do you think you'll grunt a lot, be a combination of cheerful and tough, or will you be some other way?
4. What do you think the best lunch would be for a police officer, and why?
5. Do you think karate or kung fu would be useful training for a cop? Why or why not?

# Emmie, eight years old

Eight-year-old Emmie lives in Presidio Heights with her mom, dad, little sister, and dog. She plans to live with them forever, even when she has her own career.

Asked what her parents do for work, Emmie says, "Mommy's a lawyer, and Daddy's a banker. When you're a lawyer, you work with problems people have, and you do computer work. If a problem is too big for you to handle, you just send them to court. When you're a banker, you work with money at a bank."

What will Emmie's career be? "I don't know . . . maybe a paleontologist, maybe an astronaut, maybe a scientist, maybe a scientist that studies space so I can practically be an astronaut scientist," she says. "Or maybe I'll be a ballerina or a soccer player. Oh, and maybe I'll be a fashion designer with my best friend."

Neither Emmie nor her best friend is fashionable, Emmie explains, "but I sew and she likes to draw. We were thinking that I would sew the clothes she draws."

Emmie has worked out the schedule she and her best friend will follow. "I will have to get up really early because

I think it will probably be a bit of a drive. Maybe she'll start first thing in the morning, before I get there, and she'll sketch some ideas so I can get to work right away. I would work daily and only have a little bit of time to eat lunch," she says. "I'm guessing if she did a lot, I'd have a whole stack of things to work on."

Where does Emmie's interest in paleontology come from? "Well, I like dinosaurs, and I like science," she says. "Paleontologists are like dinosaur bone scientists, so they study dinosaur bones." Emmie's favorite lesson from her science studies so far is erosion, "where the land breaks down a little bit, or a lot," she explains.

As for her desire to be an astronaut, "I like space. I think it would be really cool to discover another galaxy," she says.

Emmie is in ballet now, and she has fun with it. "Maybe the director of a show likes both ballet and tap. So if I have to, I'll do tap dance too," she says.

Soccer appeals to Emmie because, like ballet, she is in soccer now and loves it. What position does she play? "Well, I don't really know," she says. "I think I'm normally in the back. I'm not the goalie, but I think I'm back left or right." Asked whether she helps the goalie, Emmie replies, "Not really."

## Insights from the Urban Playground

San Francisco is an ideal place for dreaming big and trying out a bunch of careers. Whether your pursuits are scientific, athletic, creative, or all of these, you can develop them in this city.

Like Emmie, you can find your business partner in grade school, and you can start exploring future careers on the ballet stage and the soccer field, even when you are a kid. There are so many sports and other activities for kids to participate in, so if you are career-minded like Emmie, it is never too early to start working on your professional path.

Go for it!

1. Do you think you will keep living with your family forever?
2. Do you think your career will be more scientific, athletic, creative, or something else?
3. Which of your friends would make a good business partner for you, and why?
4. Do you have a favorite subject in school that you think would make a good career for you someday
5. Would you find it fun to discover a new galaxy?

# Graham, eight years old

Graham, an eight-year-old boy who lives in the Outer Sunset when with his mom and in Outer Parkside when with his dad, has three ideas for his future career: pro baseball or soccer player, server in a Mexican restaurant, or video game designer. Graham has one sibling, an older brother.

According to Graham, San Francisco's biggest problems are ocean pollution and people leaving the faucet running. He is happy in the city despite these issues, and says that whichever path he pursues, he will live in San Francisco when he grows up.

Graham would play third base in baseball or goalie in soccer. If he worked in a restaurant, he would be a waiter instead of the owner because serving people would be more fun than being the boss.

"I like meeting new people," he explains, "and I would get to walk around a lot and see what food other people like."

Being a video game designer would be fun because Graham could invent the game's storyline—"not how it looks, but what you do in the game," he explains. "Then when you finish making it, you get to test it, and then you could tell everyone you made it." He would work downtown, like his mom does. "I would bring mini-sandwiches or something in a thermos for lunch, like rice and meat," he says.

The job Graham would least want is house cleaner. "That is not fun, even though they get a lot of money," he says. How important is it to Graham that he earns a lot of money? "If I live by myself, pretty important," he says. "If I live with someone, not as important, but still important."

Graham's work ideas are based on his current interests: he plays baseball and flag football on teams, and soccer for fun. Mexican food is his favorite. Graham likes playing video games, board games, and the card games Bead, Garbage, and Spoon.

Graham's mom is a lawyer, and his dad "works at home for an art company," Graham says. "I think he helps with the posters or just does stuff on the computer."

Graham thinks his mom's work would be fun because "she gets to argue with people. If you're arguing with someone," he says, "and then you're right, and the judge says they're wrong, you get to tell them you are right and they are wrong. And then they know."

His dad's work would be fun, Graham says, because "he designs stuff for art, and when people buy it, they're using his product. Also, his friend is his boss."

## Insights from the Urban Playground

The Outer Sunset isn't known for its Mexican restaurants . . . yet. Who knows what it will be like once Graham enters the working world?

Playing sports, serving food to people, and designing video games may seem like unrelated goals, but Graham has chosen three fields that are thriving in San Francisco.

San Francisco people love the Giants for baseball, the 49ers for football, and the Warriors for basketball. The dining scene in San Francisco is quite something, with everyone trying new restaurants. And video games? Well, San Francisco is known for a little thing called tech. Graham is all set!

---

**DISCUSSION QUESTIONS**

1. What do you think is so bad about people leaving the faucet running in San Francisco?
2. If you were a restaurant server, what kind of food would you want to serve, and why?
3. If you were a video game designer, what would happen in the video game you would design?
4. When you go to work someday, what will you put in your thermos for lunch?
5. What do you think is fun about the work your parents do/your parent does?

# Elise, seven years old

Seven-year-old Elise, an only child living in Lower Pacific Heights with her mom and dad, wants to be an archaeologist when she grows up. "I really want to dig up dinosaur bones, and I like playing in the dirt," she explains.

Elise says her love of science and history inspires her career choice. "I like learning about famous heroes, like Frida Kahlo, Martin Luther King, and George Washington," she says.

Kahlo interests Elise because "a bus hit her," Elise says. She likes King because "he led a march that seemed cool," and Washington because he was the first president. "It was probably scary for him because people maybe didn't want to vote for him, so he worked so, so hard to be president," she says.

What does an archaeologist do all day? "Goes in the hot sun and digs up and dusts off dinosaur bones," Elise says. "After that, they get to put it in the museum, and it usually takes about maybe a month or a year to dig up one dinosaur." The hard part about being an archaeologist would be "working in the sun, pretty hot."

Elise has seen dinosaur bones at the California Academy of Sciences, one of her favorite San Francisco museums, which she likes to visit with her maternal grandparents when they come to town from Racine, Wisconsin.

Asked what will make her stand out at work, Elise responds, "I'm hardworking. I might have to dig really hard, but will probably take breaks." And what will her personality be like at work? "Happy and probably hot," she says.

It won't all be field work, though. Elise says she'll have an office to go back to after her digs, "and then I'd show the dinosaur bones I'd dug up to my boss, or I wouldn't show them to my boss because I might be the boss," she says.

Elise thinks she'll miss school once she is in the working world "because Mommy said she missed being in school instead of going to work." Elise thinks she will miss all the nice teachers at school and her family picking her up.

Elise's favorite classes are reader's workshop and writer's workshop. What is fun about reader's workshop? "I'm kind of proud because I finished a whole chapter book in a week," she answers. The book was part of the *Mermaid Tales* series, and after finishing that one, she is onto another from the set.

Elise likes writer's workshop because she gets to write her own books. She has already written "one tiny book" called *The Three Buddies* and can't wait to write more.

## Insights from the Urban Playground

San Francisco's Academy of Sciences is a fantastic museum for a budding archaeologist to visit! It has many scientific wonders to explore, dinosaur bones being just one.

And did you know that Frida Kahlo lived in San Francisco? She did! Not for long, and the city is not where she had her bus accident that Elise mentioned—but, yes, San Francisco is part of Kahlo's personal history.

San Francisco may not be the best place for archaeological digs, though people do occasionally find old animal bones, usually when a house is under renovation or other construction. But *dinosaur* bones? Maybe not.

---

1. What is something you like to play now that would make a good job for you someday?
2. What would be the best part about finding dinosaur bones?
3. What do you think you'll miss most about school when you are working?
4. Who is someone from history who inspires you?
5. If you had a class called writer's workshop, or if you do, what would/do you write?

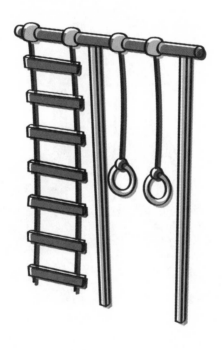

# *Acknowledgments*

To Brooke Warner, Amy Baker, Janis Cooke Newman, Sally Smith, Will Marks, Julia Scheeres, Debbie Rosenthal, Sam Jelley, Brittny Bottorff, Rose-Ellen Fairgrieve, Sarah Heegaard Rush, Shana Mahaffey, Joanna Biggar, Christi Clancy, Scott James, Johnnie Bernhard, Megan Holt, Jessica Lanning, Monya Baker, Mike Lisboa, Kerrie Smyres, Carol Salvagione, Miegan Riddle, Grazia Bennett, Audrey Murray, Nikki Shapiro, Traci Hollander, Joe Freund, Michelle Harris, Nancy Alpert, Mayra Sustaita, Kristine Stewart, Jim Argo, Chanda Nash, Steven Kamla, Tom Yankowski, Harold Holness, Supervisor Rafael Mandelman, Tari Quinn, Gerry Morales, Fernande Bencze, Laurie King, and Ivory Madison: thank you for believing in this project.

To the parents and other significant adults of the fifty San Francisco children featured in this book: thank you for sharing your kind, funny, smart, savvy, precious city kids with me.

# About the Author

Katie Burke is a San Francisco writer whose work includes Noe Kids, a monthly column for *The Noe Valley Voice*, featuring kids ages four to thirteen who live in Noe Valley. Katie has taught creative writing to children and adults in Kenya, South Africa, and San Francisco. She travels to New Orleans regularly, and her writing expresses her appreciation for San Francisco's and New Orleans' eccentric characters. Also a family law attorney, Katie writes quarterly judicial and attorney profiles for *San Francisco Attorney Magazine*. Her other publications include HarperCollins, the *L.A. Times*, and KQED *Perspectives*.

*Author photo © Steven Kamla*

# About SparkPress

SparkPress is an independent, hybrid imprint focused on merging the best of the traditional publishing model with new and innovative strategies. We deliver high-quality, entertaining, and engaging content that enhances readers' lives. We are proud to bring to market a list of *New York Times* best-selling, award-winning, and debut authors who represent a wide array of genres, as well as our established, industry-wide reputation for creative, results-driven success in working with authors. SparkPress, a BookSparks imprint, is a division of SparkPoint Studio LLC.

Learn more at GoSparkPress.com

# SELECTED TITLES FROM SPARKPRESS

SparkPress is an independent boutique publisher delivering high-quality, entertaining, and engaging content that enhances readers' lives, with a special focus on female-driven work. www.gosparkpress.com

*Potty-Mouthed: Big Thoughts for Little Brains*, Anne Johnsos. $19.95, 978-1-943006-30-4. An illustrated collection of the hilarious things kids say, collected by a couple as they stagger through the punch-in-the-gut and laugh-out-loud moments all parents experience while raising new talkers.

*Oh, What a Treat! 36 Cute & Clever Food Crafts*, Sandra Denneler. $24.95,978-1-940716-70-1. These crafts are good enough to eat! Follow along as Sandra Denneler, a graphic designer by day and food wizard by night, creates delightfully delicious recipe that you can easily recreate in your own kitchen.

*Raising a Doodle: Heartwarming Stories & Practical Tips*, Theresa Piasta. $29.95, 978-1-68463-020-2. Learn and laugh alongside puppy parents who have shared their practical tips and heartwarming stories about the joys of raising a doodle. Whether you welcomed a doodle into your life years ago, or are just now preparing to adopt a puppy, this book will help you and your fluffy best friend live a happy and healthy life together.

*Roots and Wings: Ten Lessons of Motherhood that Helped Me Create and Run a Company*, Margery Kraus with Phyllis Piano. $16.95, 978-1-68463-024-0. Margery Kraus, a trailblazing corporate and public affairs professional who became a mother at twenty-one, shares ten lessons from motherhood and leadership that enabled her to create, run, and grow a global company. Her inspiring story of crashing through barriers as she took on increasingly challenging opportunities will have women of all ages cheering.